Pyramid Power

G. PAT FLANAGAN, Ph. D.

1975

DE VORSS & CO.
1641 Lincoln Blvd.
Santa Monica, Calif. 90404

Library of Congress Catalog Card Number: 73-86022

6th Edition

ISBN 0-87516-209-6

Printed in the United States of America by
DeVorss & Co., 1641 Lincoln Blvd., Santa Monica, Calif. 90404

ACKNOWLEDGEMENT

The author would like to thank
DIMENSIONS of Los Angeles,
California, for providing much of
the material for Chapter 8 of this
book.

Each sentence in this book is a complete thought within itself, and is therefore printed in a format known as *Ventilated Prose*.

Inscription above the doorway at the Temple of Delphi:

"MAN KNOW THYSELF AND YOU WILL KNOW THE GODS AND THEIR ENERGIES."

TABLE OF CONTENTS

CONTENTS

LIST OF FIGURES

Chapter 1

AREA OF INVESTIGATION

"The possession of Knowledge, unless accompanied by a manifestation and expression in Action, is like the hoarding of precious metals—a vain and foolish thing.

Knowledge, like Wealth, is intended for use.

The LAW OF USE IS UNIVERSAL, and he who violates it suffers by reason of his conflict with natural forces."[1]

The study of life energy and life forces has gone on for thousands of years.

The idea of the existence of such energy has plagued scientists, philosophers, and religious leaders for centuries.

It is the purpose of this paper to bring up to date past concepts of these energies, and to shed new light on their qualities as a result of my own investigations.

The present investigation of these energies may correctly be ascribed to the area of Para-Physics, as many of these discoveries are on the borderline of physical and psychic phenomena.

When the experiments to be described are performed thousands of times by thousands of people and all the laws governing its origin and use are known, it may then become a part of the subject of Physics.

It is my own opinion that investigation of these energies

1

is of paramount importance to man's understanding of himself and his place as a spiritual entity in the vast reaches of the cosmos.

The bringing together of East and West, that is, the Spiritual and the Physical will bring about an uplifting of man's awareness of himself and his relationships with his brothers.

If man is to survive in peace with his fellows, he must develop a further understanding of life itself and the energies surrounding life. Then he may have a better understanding of his place in the Universe.

Chapter 2

HISTORY

In the Far East, the idea of Life Energy has been known for thousands of years.

Ga-llama

The oldest known term for this energy is GA-LLAMA.[2] This term is believed to have been originated by the ancient Egyptians, and is believed to go back 142,000 years.

GA-LLAMA is the very foundation of existence, with every indrawn breath you take on new life.

The basic qualities of GA-LLAMA are not fully known.

It is the basis of a system of YOGA known as Caucasian or Egyptian YOGA, the basic technique for increasing it is to perform certain breathing exercises.

Prana

The next reference to LIFE ENERGY is contained in ancient Sanscrit, this term still being used today in modern Hindu Yoga is called PRANA.[3]

Prana is the Sanscrit term meaning "ABSOLUTE ENERGY."

The Hindus term Prana as the universal life principle of energy or force, and that all energy or force is derived from that principle, or a particular manifestation of that principle.

3

The Hindus believe that the very air we breathe is charged with Prana.

Just as the oxygen we breathe is absorbed by the blood and used to nourish the system, so Prana is taken up by the nervous system, and is exhausted by our thinking, willing, acting, etc.

Every thought, every act, every effort of the will, every motion of a muscle, uses up a certain amount of what is called nerve force, which is believed to be a form of Prana.

All the Yoga breathing systems are based on the inflow of Prana into the body, and its distribution into the various channels in which it flows.

These channels are called Chakras, and are believed to be coincident with the endocrine glands.

It is believed that the amount of Prana taken into the body affects the AURA or energy field surrounding the body.

The YOGIS believe they can charge organic and inorganic materials with Prana by numerous means of exercises.

A technique described in the last reference is that of charging water with Prana by breathing rhythmically, holding a glass of water in the left hand, then gathering the fingers of the right hand together and shaking them gently over the water, as if you were shaking drops of water off of your fingertips into the glass.

The mental image of the Prana being passed into the water must also be held.

Water thus charged is supposed to be stimulating to weak persons expanding their aura.

4

Kundalini

Whereas the Hindus believe the air we breathe to be filled by Prana, or life energy in the air, they also believe the body to contain a more powerful form of energy called Kundalini.

"Kundalini is the individual bodily representative of the great cosmic power which creates and sustains the universe."[4]

The Yogis believe Kundalini to be a sleeping serpent at the base of the spine.

The residing place of Kundalini is known as the Muladhara Chakra.

It is visualized as a serpent with three and one half coils, representing latent energy to be released, which occurs when the sleeping serpent is awakened by pranayama breathing exercise.[5]

As the sleeping serpent is awakened and starts its ascent upward, a feeling of heat is developed at the base of the spine, as the lowest chakra becomes vivified or active.

This feeling of heat then passes upward as the Kundalini ascends and vivifies the six upper chakras terminating in the thousand petalled lotus, the Brahamaranda Chakra at the top of the head, which is connected with the pineal gland.

When the pineal gland becomes awakened and vivified, it commences to perform its normal function as a third eye for telepathic vision.

Hindu drawings of the chakras and the concept of Kundalini fire flowing from the base chakra to the topmost one are illustrated in Figure 1.

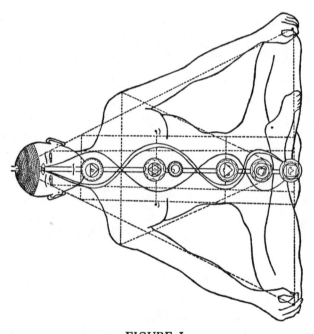

FIGURE I

The chakras of the body and the concept of the Kundalini fire extending from the base of the spine to the topmost chakra in the head.

6

Tumo

The Tibetan adepts and masters of the monasteries of northern India call the universal life energy TUMO.[6]

Tibetan adepts are able to withstand subfreezing temperatures completely naked at altitudes of 18,000 feet or more surrounded by snow.

The word TUMO signifies heat, warmth, and fire.
It is not used in the Tibetan language to express ordinary heat or warmth.

The adepts are able to generate heat of such intensity that they melt the snow for distances up to twenty feet around them.

The channels through which Tumo flows are called tsas, or rtsa which means vein, artery and nerve.

These veins correspond to the nadis of the Hindus used to convey Kundalini to the various chakras.

These so called arteries are not supposed to be true arteries containing blood, but exceedingly thin nerves that distribute currents of psychic energy.

Enlightened mystics consider the tsa system as devoid of any physical reality, but to be part of an energy body which surrounds the physical.

The Tumo initiate must perform a series of ten exercises while naked and wet at altitudes above 10,000 feet in freezing weather.

Once perfected, the initiate must renounce all fur or woolen clothing and never approach a fire to warm himself.

7

The basic exercises are as follows:

1. The central artery . . . UMA . . . is imagined, and subjectively seen, as thin as the tiniest thread of hair, yet filled with the ascending flame and crossed by the current of air produced by the breath.

2. The artery has increased in size and becomes as large as the little finger.

3. It continues to increase and appears to be the size of an arm.

4. The artery fills the whole body, or rather the body has become the tsa itself, a kind of tube filled with blazing fire and air.

5. The bodily form ceases to be perceived. Enlarged beyond all measure, the artery engulfs the whole world and the initiate feels himself to be a storm-beaten flame among the flowing waves of an ocean of fire.

This state has taken about an hour.

6. The stormy wind abates, the fiery waves sink lower and are less agitated, the blazing ocean narrows and is absorbed in the body.

7. The artery, which is reduced to the size of an arm, is seen again with fire enclosed in it.

8. The artery decreases to the size of the little finger.

9. It becomes as thin as a hair.

10. It entirely disappears: the fire ceases utterly to be perceived, as well as all forms, all representations whatsoever.

At this stage, the initiate's mind sinks into a trance of emptiness.

The whole exercise once perfected, can be practiced whenever one is cold.

The Tibetans also speak of other energies called shugs or tsal.

They believe this energy is produced every time a thought is made, or any physical action takes place.

The production of psychic phenomena depends upon the strength of that energy and the direction in which it is pointed.

The lamas claim they can charge inanimate objects with this energy, and that the objects impart it to people and other things which come in contact with it.

Tch'i

TCH'I is the name of life energy given by the ancient Chinese.

Tch'i is the vital energy which flows through all living things.

The practice of Chinese acupuncture is based on the flow of this energy through the twelve meridians of the body.[7]

Figure 10 is an example of some of the meridians of acupuncture.

These meridians correspond more or less with the tsas mentioned earlier in the section on Tumo.

The meridians of acupuncture may be detected in a number of ways by the use of modern instruments.[8]

These methods and instruments will be described in some detail in a later section of this paper.

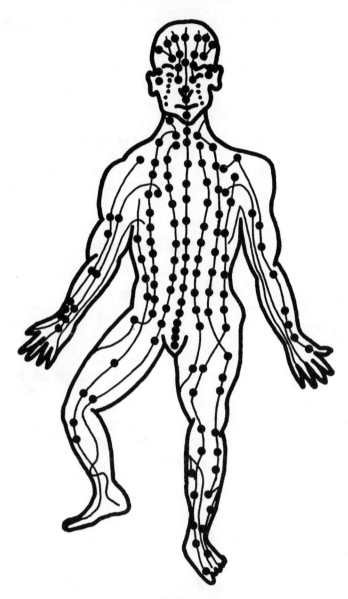

FIGURE II

A few of the many Acupuncture points which may be detected by means of Kirlian photography, voltage differentials, or by means of GSR changes.

Tch'i is also called CHI,[9] which originally meant "air" or breath.

Wang Ch'ung who lived from 27 A.D. to 95 A.D. signified it as "prime energy" which motivates the law of nature.

He said that this energy circulates throughout the entire body and regulates the circulation of the blood, digestion, and the autoprotection of the organism.

Another Chinese word for this energy is Qi or Ki.[10] Qi is usually broken down into two categories by the Chinese, the male and the female, that is, the Yang and the Yin.

It is the study of these flows throughout the entire body on which acupuncture is based.

The theory is that certain areas become deficient of energy, or become blocked or congested.

In other words, they become unbalanced.

The process of acupuncture is the rebalancing of these energies by means of massage, needles, electrical impulse, laser, or other means of precise stimulation.

Some of these techniques will be covered in later chapters.

Mana, Mana Mana, Mana Loa

The ancient Hunas of Hawaii have three names for the life energy.[11]

Mana, or body waves; Mana Mana, or thinking waves; and Mana Loa, the spiritual or psychic energy.

Mana Loa is the most highly evolved, and is the one with the most power to influence all things.

11

Mana Loa is symbolized as the sun, or provider of all life.

The Kahunas believe that we have three bodies made up of these energies, each one on a different plane of function.[12]

These bodies are called aka bodies.

The three bodies are each accompanied by the three forces:

1. Mana . . . The body waves or low voltage vital electrical force. It can carry chemical substances with it and can flow from person to person. It can take the form of magnetism and can be stored in wood and in other substances. A large discharge of this low voltage vital force, commanded by the "will" can exert a paralyzing effect, or a mesmeric effect resulting in unconsciousness, sleep and the rigid or cataleptic state.

2. Mana Mana . . . The brain waves or vital force of the next higher voltage, used by the conscious mind in all its thinking and "willing" activities.

Used as will, it can be mesmeric or hypnotic, provided that a thought form is introduced into the mind of the subject.

3. Mana Loa . . . The high voltage of vital force, is thought to be used by the superconscious for its various purposes.

It is considered to be the most powerful of all the psychic energies.

From the ancient studies and philosophies we progress through time to the western world of the fifteenth century.

Quintessence

Quintessence is the name given life energy or psychic energy by the great alchemist philosopher Paracelsus.

Paracelsus was born Philippus Aureolus Theophrastus Bombastus Paracelsus von Hohenheim.

He is better known as Paracelsus.
Paracelsus, known as the "Swiss Hermes," was born in 1490 in the Canton of Schwyz.

He is one of the fathers of modern medicine.[13]
Paracelsus considered this energy to fill the whole universe and to be the magnetic light force which is the basis of all things.

It is believed that Paracelsus succeeded in the impossible, that of transmuting other lesser metals into gold.

Od or Odic Force

In the early 19th century, the great chemist, Baron Karl von Reichenbach discovered what he called the Od or Odic Light Force.[14]

Reichenbach, an outstanding authority on meteorites, the discoverer of parafin, the inventor of creosote and pitacol was one of the great scientists of Europe.

Reichenbach became interested in people he called human barometers.

These people were very sensitive to weather conditions, and could detect the onset of electrical storms and other disturbances well in advance.

He discovered that these individuals were able to detect magnetic fields and were able to "see" these fields around magnets and various crystal shapes.

13

One end of a magnet was said to be cold, and blue in color; the North seeking pole.

The other end was said to be red in color, and hot.

The sensitives said that they could see the fields of the human body and described these in great detail.

The sensitives were able to detect without error the poles of magnets and crystals repeatedly using only their super senses.

They were able to describe the way the energies in all things affected each other.

Reichenbach used a great number of people in his experiments and was very careful to make sure none of his subjects knew each other.

All the results correlated exactly from one sensitive to the next.

Reichenbach wrote several books on the subject.

On the Nature of Odic Light

Odic Light exhibits the same laws and phenomena as ordinary visible light.[15]

Odic Light may appear in connection with all objects, but more especially when these objects are under the influence of fine forces such as electricity, heat, light, and magnetism.

When Reichenbach placed metal plates in the sunlight, with a wire running from the plate into a dark room, sensitives saw Odic flames appear on the end of the wire in the darkened room. The psychics could tell instantly when an assistant unknown to them would remove the plates from sunlight.

14

Magnetized water was detected without error from water which had not been treated with magnetic fields, although no instruments were available to Reichenbach to measure Odic Light.

Reichenbach used the best means to ensure an exact experimental scientific approach to his investigations.

Reichenbach is the first major western scientist to investigate these energies.

The first recorded attempt I know of to build an instrument to measure these energies is a device illustrated in Figure III.[16]

This device has also been called a Sthenometer.

It is basically a very fine balanced needle suspended by a fine silk thread over a calibrated dial.

The entire unit is then suspended in a glass shield preferably made of quartz.

It is claimed that the device will respond instantly to the visual stimulus of the gaze, and to the proximity of the human body.

We shall see later that a similar device has been used by the Russians in their research.

A device of my own creation will also be described.

Mitogenic Rays

In the late 1930's, Dr. Alexander Gurvich, a Russian scientist, announced to the world an astounding discovery. That all living cells produce an invisible radiation.

He called this new discovery mitogenic radiation.[17]

15

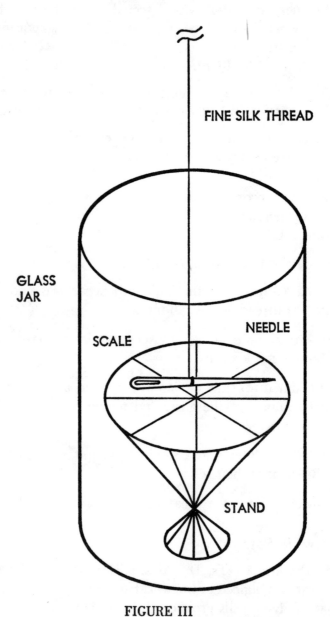

FINE SILK THREAD

GLASS
JAR

SCALE

NEEDLE

STAND

FIGURE III

Early form of psychic detector called a Sthenometer.

Gurvich claimed these radiations were similar in nature to ultraviolet rays.

In 1930, Professor Guido Cremonese succeeded in photographing these rays. He published his photographs in a paper entitled *I Raggi della vita fotografati.*

Gurvich claimed that small roots of freshly cut vegetables radiated mitogenic rays as long as the nucleus is not destroyed.

Gurvich chose the root of a freshly sprouted onion as the "sender" and mounted the root in a tube like a "biological cannon." [18]

He pointed the root tip at another onion root, the "receiver," also in a tube but with an area exposed on its side.

After three hours, Gurvich counted the number of cells in the exposed area of the receiver and the number of cells on the side not exposed.

There were twenty-five percent more cells in the area exposed to the biological shooter.

He tried placing sheets of quartz between the sender and the receiver and obtained the same results.

He tried yeast as a receiver and obtained a thirty percent increase in growth.

In humans, Gurvich discovered that muscle tissue, the cornea of the eye, blood, and nerves were all shooters of what he called mitogenic rays.

Scientists at a French hospital found that when sick people held a culture of yeast in the hand the radiations were changed and killed the yeast whereas a normal person increased yeast growth.

Gurvich formulated the theory of a biological force field but his discovery was lost in time until recently.

His early work we shall later see is a very important discovery leading to the theory of biological plasma or bioplasma as the Russians now call this energy.

Bioplasma

In 1939, a Soviet electrician, Semyon Davidovich Kirlian discovered a phenomenon which is now called Kirlian Photography.

He discovered that the human body, indeed all living things could be made to radiate energy which could be photographed by external stimulation of the body by means of high frequency high voltage alternating current.

The rays appear to follow certain definite lines of force and vary according to mood, health, and emotional activity.

The Russians called this field of energy Bioplasmic energy, a sort of cold plasma surrounding all living things.[18]

A typical Kirlian setup is shown in Figure IV.

The Kirlian photography apparatus is basically a high frequency oscillator anywhere from 100,000 cycles to 4,000,000 cycles per second.

The device produces voltages from 20,000 to 100,000 volts peak to peak.

By means of various electrodes, a whole new world of color and form comes into view.

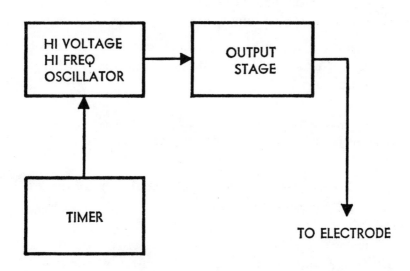

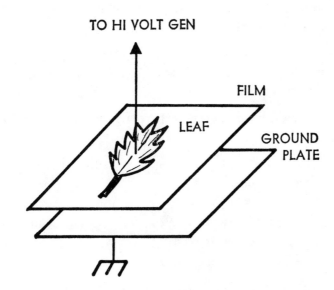

FIGURE IV

Kirlian photography set-up.

19

Multicolored flames, flares, sparks, twirls, and twinkles, all in motion like a million Roman candles all at once.

A freshly cut leaf showed a whole panorama of intense energy: after several hours, the leaf appeared as though it was turning off its lights.

The Kirlian system soon became one of the most important tools the Russians had in the investigation of life energy.

Several Kirlian photographs will be shown in the experimental section of this report.

Through Kirlian photography, Soviet scientists discovered the shape and pattern characteristics of the energy fields surrounding all living things.

They were able to see the living moving double energy body of the things, the aura in its living glory.

The Soviets described the field as an elementary plasma-like constellation made of ionized excited electrons, protons, and other particles.

The energy body appeared to be a whole unified organism in itself.

It acted as a unit, and the Russians claim it is the basis of all biological fields.

Soviet scientists claim that oxygen from the air contains the energy which is transformed into the bioplasmic body.

This bears a striking resemblance to the descriptions of energy from the air in the breathing exercises in the oriental prana theories.

20

The Soviets say that deep breathing recharges the entire bioplasmic body and helps to equalize disturbed energy patterns.

Soviet scientists discovered this is the reason breathing negatively charged ionized air was very effective in relieving tension and tiredness.

They discovered that different colors of light affect the pattern of discharge of the bioplasmic body.

The various researchers agree on the following characteristics of vital energy:

It could be reflected, refracted, polarized, and combined with other energies.

It could create effects similar to magnetism, electricity, heat, and luminous radiations, but was in itself none of these.

It was said that this odd energy from humans could be conducted by paper, wood, wool, silk, and many substances that are electrical insulators.

Pyramid Power

In the late 1930's, a Frenchman by the name of Bovis was visiting the Great Pyramid of Gizeh while on a holiday.

While Bovis was in the King's Chamber he noticed a garbage can filled to the top with small dead animals.

He found small cats, dogs, mice, and other rodents completely mummified with no trace of decay or putrefaction.

When Bovis asked the keeper of the pyramid about the dead animals, he replied that small animals and

21

rodents wander into the pyramid from time to time and get lost in its vast structure.

When they can not find their way out again the small animals eventually starve to death.

The pyramid keepers find the small bodies and place them in a garbage can for keeping until the can fills up, at which point they go bury the contents and start with a new can.

This process has been going on in the pyramid for thousands of years.[18]

Bovis noticed that there was no odor of decay.
He picked up one of the small cats in the can and it was completely mummified with no sign of putrefaction.

Bovis examined several of the small animals and discovered that all of them were completely preserved.

The problem of the mummified animals began to bother Bovis.

As soon as he was back from his trip he decided to perform an experiment with the shape of the pyramid. He built a three foot base plywood pyramid and placed a freshly dead cat in the section corresponding to the King's chamber.

In a few days Bovis had a perfectly mummified cat with no sign of decay.

He then began a series of painstaking experiments in earnest.

Bovis placed various perishable food items in the pyramid and placed controls on the outside of the structure.

Many of the items were things that spoil very easily such as brain tissue, liver, eggs, and hamburger meat.

In all cases he reported no spoilage on items placed in the pyramid.

All his controls had to be thrown out because of decay.

Bovis published his findings, but was not taken seriously by the majority of his readers.

A *few* people did take him seriously, in the United States, and behind the iron courtain.

In Italy, a milk company packages all its milk in pyramid shaped containers.

The company claims its milk will keep indefinitely with no refrigeration.[19]

Karel Drbal, a Czechoslovakian radio engineer, read Bovis' report and decided to experiment with the pyramid shape to determine what he could about this strange energy.

Drbal duplicated Bovis' experiments and went off on his own into uncharted territory.

A major problem in the communist countries is the availability of good razor blade steel.

Russian soldiers only get one razor blade a month and it does not last more than one or two shaves.

Where there is a need, there is a way.

Drbal wondered if this mysterious energy might have an effect on razor blades.

23

As a younger man he had been in the army and recalled tricks his friends would play on each other.

They would steal each other's blades at night and place them on the window sill in the moon light so that the polarized rays from the moon would fall on the blades.

By morning the blades would be dull with no physical evidence they had been tampered with.

Drbal wondered what the pyramid power would do to the blade.

He shaved with a blade several times and then placed the blade inside a small six inch base pyramid made of cardboard.

After a time, he tested the blade and discovered that it was sharp again.

He continued to place the blade under the pyramid between shaves and discovered he could shave 200 times with a single blade!

Soon all his friends were sharpening their blades under a pyramid.

Word soon spread and Soviet soldiers started building their own pyramid razor blade sharpeners.

At the insistence of friends, Drbal applied for a patent on his pyramid razor blade sharpener.

After much quibbling, he received Czech patent number 91304 entitled "Cheops Pyramid Razor Blade Sharpener."

Drbal had no idea what happened to the blade in the pyramid but he had a theory that the crystal structure of the blade was deformed by the process of shaving and that the pyramid energy had the effect of rejuvenating this structure as long as the blade was not physically damaged.

Psychotronic Energy

Czech scientists have been hard at work investigating pyramid power and other forms of "shaped power."

A Czech engineer, Robert Pavlita has come up with a number of interesting devices he calls "psychotronic generators."

These devices resemble modern art sculpturings made of metal, wood, and paper.[18]

At least one American scientist has visited Pavlita and examined his generators and could detect no fraud.[20]

It is claimed that the various generators can create mechanical movement, purify water, and attract magnetic and non magnetic particles, even under water!

The Czechs have been very hush hush about the devices and have revealed nothing that can be evaluated properly.

It would appear that the pyramid shape is a clue to these devices.

I was informed of a standing order that was in effect during World War II to all American pilots stationed in Egypt.

All pilots were told not to fly over the Great Pyramid because the instruments went haywire if they did.

I interviewed one pilot who did, and he said his instruments stopped working completely.

Apparently lower insects cannot stand this energy.

One person reported that maggots left meat if a pyramid was placed over the maggot infested meat.

He said the maggots left and starved to death rather than go back to the meat.

Chapter 3

AUTHOR'S BACKGROUND, THE NEUROPHONE

In 1958, when I was fourteen years old, a close friend of mine, Lou Macko, a television repairman in Houston, Texas told me of a most unusual phenomenon.

He told me of a device that would transmit sound to the brain without using the ears.

The description of the device had been given to him by a complete stranger when he had visited Chicago.

The device consisted of two copper mesh scrub pads with wires attached to them.

The pads were placed in a pair of plastic bags to act as insulators.

The wires were then connected to the high voltage side of an audio output transformer which was connected back-to-back with the output of an ordinary record player.

The result is shown in Figure V.

The voltage from the Hi Fi was stepped up a bit and applied to the pads.

If the pads were placed on the skin of the head in the vicinity of the temples, one would "hear" the sound from the Hi Fi as if it were coming from within the head itself.

The item at that time had no practical advantage as it was extremely distorted.

A good deal of the sound seemed to be missing as if it were cut off.

I researched at the library and discovered the phenomenon was known as far back as 1800 and was discovered by Volta.

It was called electrophonic hearing.

It was believed that the phenomenon was merely the action of the muscles being electrically stimulated and affecting the bones in the ear by means of minute muscle vibration.

I examined the signal from the device by oscilloscope and discovered the sound came through in a blast when the transformer was overloaded and produced a sharp spike or ringing on the wave form.

I soon discovered that the real information was coming through only when this effect occurred.

This explained why only parts of the music and voice came through.

I reasoned that the true carrier of information was a radio signal due to the oscillation produced by shock excitation of the combined circuit of the transformer and the parallel tuned circuit formed by the electrodes and the human body.

I started experimenting with the unit using a high frequency oscillator of my own design and discovered a resonance in the circuit around 40,000 cycles per second.

I soon found that the resonant frequency would change abruptly with emotions and general body changes.

The capacitance of the electrodes, therefore the dielectric constant of the skin, changed abruptly from the slightest outside stimulus.

The dielectric constant of the skin would change by several orders of magnitude in a fraction of a second!

The experimental arrangement for measuring resonance is illustrated in Figure VI.

After preliminary measurement of parameters, I designed the original Neurophone which is illustrated in my patent on the device.

The device was essentially a high voltage frequency modulated radio transmitter of low power.

Its frequency was adjustable to correct for changes of resonance.

The original unit was hand adjustable. Later units were automatically tuned for maximum resonance.

The addition of the resonant radio carrier wave made the difference.
The sound from the device was fantastic, like sound from another world.

The normal frequency response of the ear was extended beyond normal boundaries and there was no distortion.

I began experimenting with a number of people who were considered to be totally nerve deaf, that is, they were unable to hear anything, even with what is known as bone conduction.

The results were spectacular.

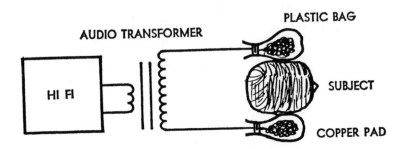

FIGURE V

Early experimental Neurophone.

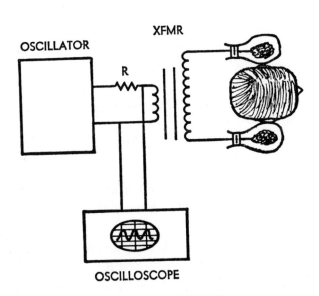

FIGURE VI

Measuring resonance.

People who had not heard in years were now hearing sounds they only dreamed of ever recapturing.

A patent was applied for, and my research continued.

The press learned of my discovery and articles appeared on the front pages of 300 newspapers, and it was picked up by news syndicates and international magazines around the world.

LIFE did an article in September of 1962.

The results were as spectacular as the discovery. We received hundreds of thousands of letters from all over the world. Letters came from as far away as Tasmania addressed only to Pat Flanagan, Inventor, Texas, U.S.A.

The U. S. Postal service did a spectacular job in getting the mail to the right party.

There were many Neurophone discoveries not made public.

On occasions the device stimulated perfect telepathic contact between one or more persons, often with startling results.

I had read many books on the subject, and had practiced Yoga from the age of eight; and now we were witnessing a new phenomenon—electronically induced telepathy.

These telepathic incidents were kept under wraps for fear of ridicule.

Aura Photography

One evening I was working in my photographic darkroom while listening to music over the Neurophone.

I often listened to music with the device as it produced the most pleasant sensation of "hearing" through the nerves, as it were.

When I developed a print from my enlarger, I discovered an outline of what appeared to be a finger on the paper.

It had lines of energy surrounding it in a sort of halo.

I tried another print and got the same results.

I then switched the Neurophone off and the finger picture disappeared.

I turned the unit back on, laid my finger on the paper and got another print surrounded by an AURA!

A copy of the print is shown in Figure VII.

On further experimentation with leaves from plants, and other living things I became convinced that I had made another discovery, a method of photographing the long sought AURA described in occult texts.

I soon discovered the energy changed in much the same way the dielectric skin constant changed, that is, according to mood, food, and state of the emotions.

Later I read reports from the Soviet Union on the subject of Kirlian Photography and was very pleased to learn that the system was also in use in other areas.

From my own research, I believe the mechanism involved in Kirlian photography is one of the stimulated emission of ultraviolet rays from the body when it is excited by high frequency, high voltage resonant signals coupled to the body.

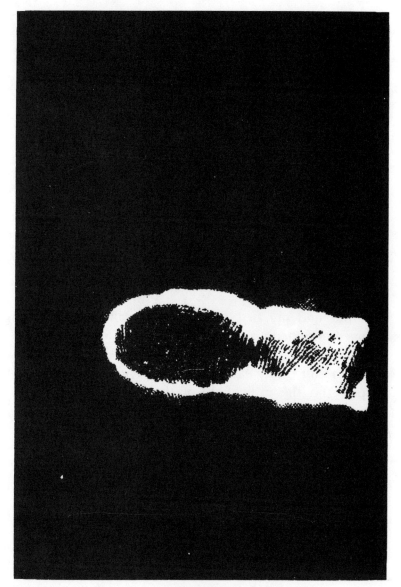

FIGURE VII

Kirlian photograph of finger.

The above photograph is similar in nature to the original photograph of my finger taken with the NEUROPHONE in 1959.

There is an excitation of "mitogenic" radiation by the dissociation of atoms on the skin's surface.

These rays then follow the lines of force surrounding the body.

The lines of force form a complex matrix around the body which the Russians call the bioplasmic body.

These lines of force are also coincident with the described aura known to the mystery schools of the Far East.

At last we had a tool for "seeing" these energies.

By measuring the brightness of the UV radiation thus stimulated, one could get a quantitative readout of the relative strengths of energy in a living organism.

I thus had my first device for measuring bio-energy or biocosmic energy as I now call it.

As a result of my early experience with Kirlian photography and the radio field of the Neurophone as well as the occasional stimulation of telepathy, I became intensely interested in the effects of the various energy fields surrounding man.

I made an intensive study of the electrical field around and on the human body, the changes in dielectric constant of the skin, the changes in resistance of acupuncture points, and the various voltage differentials present on the surface of the body.

I was convinced that man's body is a complex integrated electronic system.

The following is a brief description of some of these

measurements as well as some of the equipment devised to measure these things.

1. *Dielectric Skin Constant*: Figure VI shows the basic test set up for measuring the changes of dielectric skin constant by changes in resonance of a tuned circuit using the body as a live dielectric constant of the capacitor circuit.

By measuring the frequency of resonance in open air and on the body, standard electronic formulas will reveal the dielectric constant of the body.

The dielectric constant changes over a very wide range depending on emotions.

In one test, I drank one ounce of pure amino acids and my body capacitance changed from 100 picofarads to 0.1 microfarad in three minutes!

There are instantaneous changes that occur with thinking, very similar to changes in GSR.

2. *GSR Measurements*: Figure VIII is a circuit diagram of an instrument for measuring GSR changes in the body of man and in plants.

This device is very sensitive to any change in the system and is adjustable from short circuit to open circuit.

Early experiments with the device indicated a drastic change in resistance when the electrodes were placed on acupuncture points.

This system is used by the Russians to detect these points.[8]

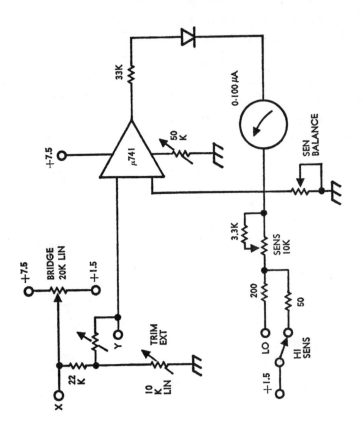

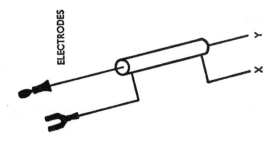

FIGURE VIII

GSR measuring bridge.

Depending on the size of the electrodes, the resistance of the skin will change from 1,000,000 ohms to as little as 2,000 ohms when correct acupuncture points are found.

The Russian counterpart of this device is called a "tobiscope."[18]

As we will see later, this device can be used for detecting biocosmic energy when it is used with a live entity as a readout sensor.

The tobiscope is basically a very sensitive Wheatstone bridge adjusted to detect changes in skin resistance.

The unit used only for acupuncture points can be simplified considerably.

It can be made to emit a loud beep when an acupuncture point is found.

The unit is used as follows: The electrodes can be used in two ways, (1) bilateral and (2) unilateral.

In the bilateral mode, the electrodes are usually two small balls on the ends of test instrument type probes.

In this mode, a test is made to determine the changes in resistance of the body from identical locations on either side, say two identical acupuncture points on the right and left sides.

The Chinese and Russians claim that there is a semiconductor effect from one side of the body to the next, that is there is a change in resistance between two points depending on the polarity of the electrodes.

As the polarity is switched the differential in skin resistance between those points is determined by the amount of unbalance of TCH'I in the body circuits.

37

When the flow of energy is balanced, there is no change in polarity.

This technique of measurement is often used to determine the amount of unbalance in the meridians of acupuncture.

The patient is then treated until the meridians are balanced.[22]

In the unilaterial mode of operation, one electrode is clipped to the ear, and the other one, the ball electrode is run over the surface of the body in search of the acupuncture point of interest.

The acupuncture points are only one millimeter in diameter and are very hard to find without this instrument.

The Chinese have catalogued over 1,000 of these points.[9]

Skin Voltage Differential

Using electrodes described in the GSR instrument, a sensitive differential volt meter can be used to chart the energy flows of the body.

The voltage range of interest is in the 0-100 mv range.

The bilateral semiconductor effect is again observed, this time as a change in polarity from side to side depending on the unbalance.

Static Voltage Field Around Body

There also exists around all living things a static voltage field.

This field changes with conditions and can be affected by the mind.

A static field intensity meter of simple design is shown in Figure IX.

This unit measures the relative values of field intensity around the body and in the atmosphere.

It shows potential as well as polarity.

The unit can be easily calibrated.

The instrument is basically an electronic electroscope with an air capacitor probe.

This device can be used to measure the effects of bio energy on living and non living things as we will describe later.

With the proper outboard equipment and filters, this instrument can pick up the heartbeat of a person due to the changes in the static field around the body.

With a device of this sort, the heartbeat can be picked up as far away as three feet.

Magnetic Field Around the Body

The body also has a magnetic field around it which can also be measured.

The equipment required is very elaborate and expensive. Only great pain or emotional stress can create enough change to be detected with an ordinary compass needle.

In times of stress the magnetic field of the body can approximate that of the earth.

An experiment can easily be performed to demonstrate this.

I have done it but it is not for the squeamish.

39

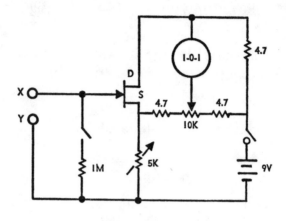

ELECTRONIC ELECTROSCOPE

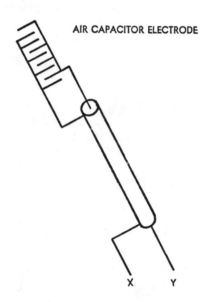

AIR CAPACITOR ELECTRODE

FIGURE IX

40

The person to be measured is to lie down on his back on the floor.

An ordinary magnetic compass is suspended over the solar plexus region of the body a few inches above.

If the subject is then given pain, as in a severe pinch, the compass needle will deflect considerably.

The effect is most strongly noted in the area of the solar plexus.

Soviet scientists have measured the field around psychics and have found vast changes in this field as certain psychic phenomena are performed.[23]

From the previous discussion, it is readily apparent that the bodies of living things are surrounded by a living, moving, biologically complex field structure.

My interest in the electronic fields of the human body expanded into the effects of the environment upon the body.

Man is living in a sea of energy of which he is not usually aware.

Our own body senses are very limited compared with the energies around us.

We are surrounded by electrostatic, magnetic, light, gravitational and other fields of which we are not normally aware.

In light energy, we are only aware of less than 0.01% of the total available light which surrounds us.

How do these unperceived fields affect our sensitive semiconductor bodies?

What affects do these fields have on basic life processes?

The most observable fields surrounding us are the magnetic fields of the Earth, and the electrostatic field gradient from the ionosphere to the surface.

Magnetic Field

The magnetic field of the earth averages about 0.5 Gauss and has a particular configuration, intensity, and mode of behavior.

It is subject to continuous pulsations of low magnitude at frequencies ranging from O.1 to 100 cycles per second, with major components at 8 to 16 cycles per second.

Any psychology text will inform us that the average frequencies of brain waves fall precisely in this range.

This falls into the area of biological entrainment of the human brain of low frequency radiation.

As the Neurophone activates the acoustic sensors of the brain, perhaps the pulsating magnetic field of the earth stimulates the normal brain rhythm.

Electrostatic Field of the Earth

The earth is surrounded by a high voltage electric field.[25]

This field extends from the ionosphere to the surface and the potential difference is between 300,000 and 400,000 volts.

The earth's surface is negatively charged, the atmosphere

is positively charged except in certain areas as in thunder storms.

The charge on the earth is generated and maintained by the action of high voltage atomic particles called cosmic rays and the action of short wave ultra-violet light emitted by the sun.

During solar flares the output of these rays can be tremendous and produce magnetic storms on the earth.

These storms have vast effects on the earth and on life.

The existence of this field has been known since 1752.

The positive field produces a voltage gradient across the atmosphere.

This gradient approaches 200 to 300 volts per meter near the surface of the earth.

This voltage can be as high as several thousand volts per meter depending on humidity, storms, etc.

Experiments have shown that this field is an important factor affecting life.

It has been shown that plants deprived of this field do not grow properly.

Plants whose seeds are sprouted in a high intensity field of this type sprout some four days earlier and grow three times as fast as plants in a low energy electrostatic field.[24]

A diagram of this energy field and the field around a man's body are shown in Figure X.

The reason we do not feel this field is that our bodies

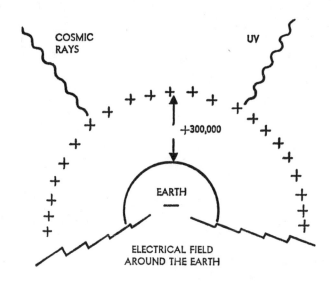

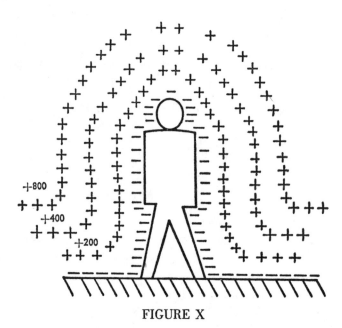

FIGURE X

Distortion of earth's field around the body of a man, note similarity to fields described as auras.

are at ground potential and the field tends to warp and distort itself around the body as shown in the diagram.

It is interesting to note that the shape of the field is the same as the shape of fields described by mystics as the aura.

The shape of this field can be measured with the electronic electroscope shown in Figure IX.

It is interesting to note that the polarity of the field around the body is sometimes changed by certain illnesses.[24]

A circuit equivalent of this field is diagrammed in Figure XI.

The total energy flowing to the earth at any given moment is 400,000 volts times the leakage current of 1800 amps or a total of 700,000,000 watts.

There are 300 thunderstorms going on at all times all over the earth.

It is believed that these storms maintain the equilibrium of the charge on the earth by maintaining the voltage difference.

The structures in which we live alter and shape this field as do our bodies.

Our modern metal buildings tend to be a Faraday cage and completely eliminate the effects of this natural field.[24]

It has been shown by research that elimination or reversal of this field can have negative effects on people augmenting fatigue, irritability, and natural apathy.[26]

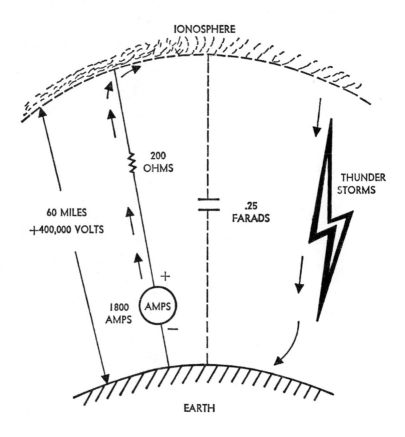

FIGURE XI

Equivalent circuit of earth's electrostatic voltage field.

Recent tests have shown that an artificially produced field of this type as high as 10,000 volts per meter has the effect of eliminating fatigue, and improving brightness discrimination.[25]

These fields increase the rate of spontaneous electrical impulse generation by the nerves.

One theory of sleep and wakefulness is based on the number of electrical impulses reaching the brain at any one time.

The beneficial effects of this field are apparently due to the combined action of the positive field and suspended negative ions in the air.

Most tests run on the effects of negative ions in the air were run without regard to the establishment of the proper voltage field to go along with the ions.

Tests run on the effects of negative ions in a proper electrostatic field have all been favorable.

The table which follows gives the gross results of the tests run by NASA:

ITEM	NEGATIVE IONS	POSITIVE IONS
Performance	Improved	Decreased
Work Capacity	Increased	
Disposition	Cheerful	Depressed
Reaction time	Decreased	Increased
Equilibrium	Improved	
Vitamin Metabolism	Enhanced	
Pain	Relieved	
Allergic Disorders	Relieved	
Burn Recovery and Healing	Enhanced	

47

Molecules of oxygen form negative ions, the positive ions are formed by carbon dioxide molecules.

This brings us back to the theory of prana and energy from the breath.

Raymond Bernard,[5] postulates that the energy from the air or prana, is due to the negative ions in the air.

Ark of the Covenant

The Ark of the Covenant is described in Exodus 25:10-21 as being a large box made of acacia wood and lined inside and out with a layer of pure gold.

The description of the Ark is of a very large electric capacitor.

If an Ark as described was built and placed in the earth's electrostatic field and charged, it would have a charge of some 600 to 1000 volts and would have enough stored charge to kill anything that touched it.

The Ark is supposed to have had the power to kill, by some mysterious energy.

I believe it killed by an electric charge.

The size of the Ark is exactly the same as the coffer in the King's chamber of the Pyramid of Gizeh.

Chapter 4

PYRAMID RESEARCH

I read with great interest the report by Bovis describing his discovery of the mummifying power of the shape of the Great Pyramid.

Having been experimenting and measuring bio-energy with the Neurophone and various other instruments described earlier, I began a series of intensive experiments on the shape of the Great Pyramid to see if I could discover its great secrets.

I began by duplicating Bovis' experiments with pyramids of various dimensions.
Using Kirlian photography, GSR, voltage differential, and electrostatic fields, I was able to measure the differences of various pyramids and their effects on living organisms such as plants and people.

The very first experiments were in the area of preserving hamburger meat, liver, eggs, and milk.
The first experiments were very encouraging.

It was strange to realize I had taken small pieces of cardboard and made a simple shape that could concentrate some sort of energy that would mummify food without any external power source.
My controls all got so bad I had to throw them away.

Bovis and Drbal had indicated in their reports that the energy was focused in the King's Chamber level

49

about one third up from the base in the middle of the pyramid.

My own research indicates that the energy is present throughout the pyramid.

I was able to mummify food anywhere in the pyramid.

By careful measurement, I was able to determine that the maximum concentration of effect was in the King's Chamber, but there were effects in the other areas of the whole pyramid.

Further research with various materials of construction revealed further clues as to the nature of the phenomenon we were investigating.

A series of energy measuring machines will be described.

Some of these machines measure the effects of the energy on other things, others are esoteric machines which are extremely sophisticated dowsing devices that rely on the human computer as a readout detector.

I have tried various other geometric shapes other than the pyramid and have not had the results obtained with the exact shape of the Pyramid of Gizeh

Other geometric structures such as cones, icosahedrons, dodecahedrons, tetrahedrons, octahedrons, greater stellated dodecahedrons, etc. all have shape characteristics, but these other shapes do not have any effects demonstrated by the exact pyramid shape to be described.

A mathematical description of the basis of geometry of the Pyramid of Gizeh follows.

Chapter 5

MATHEMATICS OF THE GREAT PYRAMID

The Great Pyramid of Gizeh is a precise mathematical structure based on the mathematical ratio of PHI (Φ), and PI (π).

Since PI can be accurately stated in terms of PHI, we shall base our mathematics on PHI (Φ).

The Sacred Cut or Golden Section

PHI is an unending ratio as is PI.

The mystical number is as old as history.

What is known as normal phylotaxis or leaf distribution in plants is represented by a curious system of numbers known as a summation series; also called the Fibonacci series.

The succeeding terms beginning with the lowest whole number are obtained by adding together the two preceeding terms.

Thus: 1, 2, 3, 5, 8, 13, 21, 34, 55, 89, 144, 233, 377, 610, 987, 1597, 2584 . . . etc.

This produces the ratio of PHI or 1.618033989 . . . etc; which is obtained by dividing any one term of the summation series by its predecessor.

The higher the terms, the closer the ratio to PHI.

FOR EXAMPLE:

1	2/1	=2.0000000
2	3/2	=1.5000000
3	5/3	=1.6666666
5	8/5	=1.6000000
13	13/8	=1.6250000
21	21/13	=1.6153846
34	34/21	=1.6190476
55	55/34	=1.6176470
89	89/55	=1.6181818
144	144/89	=1.6179775
233	233/144	=1.6180555
377	377/233	=1.6180257
610		

The series continues on and on.

PHI is also known as the SACRED CUT.

This is represented by the fact that it is the exact ratio in which we can divide a line AC by B in such a manner that $AC/AB=1.618..$

This magic ratio was used in the Renaissance by all the great Masters and is considered to be the most aesthetic proportion of division.

The body of man is divided by this ratio.

The sacred five pointed star's diagonals divide each other by this ratio.

These proportions occur throughout nature.

PI expressed in terms of PHI is as follows:

$$\emptyset = 0.5 + \frac{\sqrt{2}}{2}$$

$$\emptyset^2 = \emptyset + 1$$

$$\pi = \emptyset^2 \times 6/5$$

THEREFORE:

$$1.61803389^2 = 2.61803399 \times 1.2 =$$

$$3.14160788$$

$$\% \ error = 0.0015\%!$$

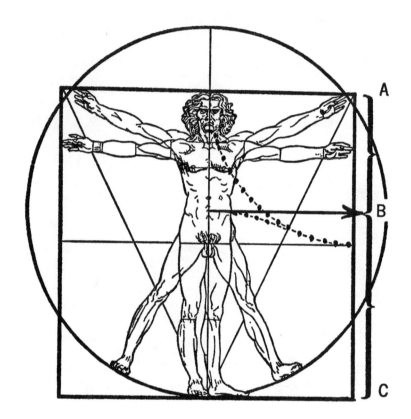

FIGURE XII

The above study by Leonardo Da Vinci shows the golden section as a basis of measurement on the human body.

The sacred proportion appears throughout nature, and is the governing ratio in the great pyramid.

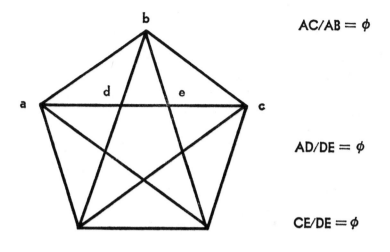

AC/AB $= \phi$

AD/DE $= \phi$

CE/DE $= \phi$

FIGURE XIII

The pentagon, and five pointed star are divided in the proportion of the golden section.

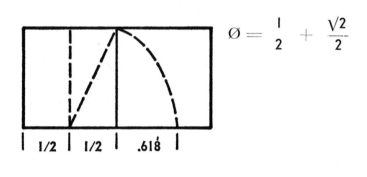

$$\emptyset = \frac{1}{2} + \frac{\sqrt{2}}{2}$$

1.618 $= \phi$

FIGURE XIV

Construction of the golden section by means of two squares and a compass.

55

Some Measurements of the Great Pyramid[28]

Original height ....5,813″
Base measurement, one face ....9,131″
Actual height, by destruction ....5,496″
Edge, face, corner to apex ....8,684″
Apothem, center of base to face of apex ....7,387″
Base angle, face to ground ....51°17′14″
Apex, interfacial angle ....76°17′32″
Edge to ground level.................................41°59′50″
Dihedral angle, face to face, edge ....106°54′
Apex, edge to edge ....96°
Circuit of the base ....36,524.24″

One terrestrial year equals 365.24 days!

Sum of base diagonals ....25,827″

The precession of our equinox is 25,827 years!

Volume of the pyramid ....90,000,000 ft³
Area covered ....13 square acres
Weight ....5,955,000 TONS

The number five appears throughout the pyramid: five sides, five corners.

The temperature inside the King's Chamber is 68° Fahrenheit.

This is exactly one fifth the distance mercury is raised in a tube between freezing and the boiling point of water at Sea Level.

This is also the optimum temperature for health and long life.

One half the base of the Pyramid divided into the apothem is equal to PHI (Φ).

For example:

$$7387/4565.5 = 1.6180374$$
$$9131/2 = 4565.5$$

Compared to the base, the edge length of the face of the Pyramid is 4.9% less: $8684/9131 = 0.9509998$.

The height of the Pyramid is 36.4% less than the base: $5813/9131 = 0.6366224$.

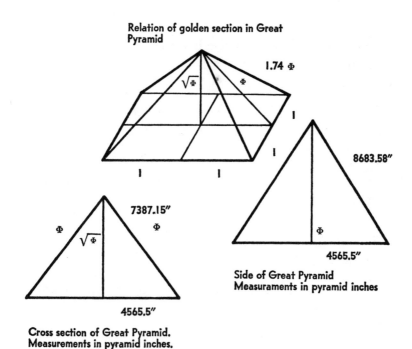

Relation of golden section in Great Pyramid

Cross section of Great Pyramid. Measurements in pyramid inches.

Side of Great Pyramid Measuraments in pyramid inches

The Great Pyramid is aligned perpendicular to True North with an error of only 4′ 32″ of one degree.[19]

See Figure XV

It is level over a thirteen acre area within one half of one inch.

The Pyramid of Gizeh is the world's largest jigsaw puzzle.

It is made of 2,6000,000 blocks of granite and limestone, each one is cut precisely for its own location in the pyramid.

The granite blocks in the King's Chamber weigh 600 tons and are polished to an accuracy of 0.001 inch over a twenty foot area.

The blocks are so hard they require two tons of pressure on a diamond bit drill to even make a dent.

The outer surface of the pyramid was covered over an area of some 21 acres by a seven foot thick layer of mirror polished pure white alabaster limestone.

The Pyramid of Gizeh is the only pyramid of its kind in the world.

It is the only one found that had ventilation shafts leading into the chambers.

There are four shafts in the pyramid, two leading the Queen's chamber, and two leading to the King's Chamber.[29]

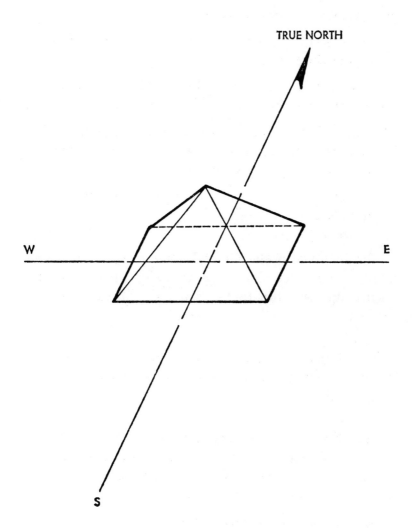

FIGURE XV

Alignment of the Great Pyramid of Gizeh.

The shafts lead from the North and South faces of the pyramid into the chambers.

The King's coffer is exactly the same size as the Biblical Ark of the Covenant.

The coffer is 89.90568 inches long, 38.69843 inches wide and 41.21319 inches high in its exterior measurements.

The sum of the length, width, and height of the coffer is equal to 1/5 of the sum of the length, width, and height of the King's Chamber itself.

The sides are close to six inches thick and the bottom seven inches.

The builders of the Great Pyramid apparently knew more of the exact dimensions of the earth than modern science up until the International Geophysical Year of 1957-1958.

The French meter, the standard measurement in Europe, the metric system standard, is based on the size of the earth.

The French meter was arrived at by taking one 10,000,000th part of the quadrant of the earth as calculated from the North Pole to the Equator, along the meridian passing through Dunkirk.

As the earth is not a perfect sphere, the said distance is not a true quadrant, hence it is not truly scientific to determine a unit of straight measure from such a surface.

If we divide the earth's polar radius by the Egyptian Sacred Cubit, we get the figure of 10,000,000 exactly!

Hence the pyramid inch is the 500,000,000th part of the earth's polar diameter.

Thus the designer of the Great Pyramid long forestalled modern man in having a unit of measure based on the size of the earth, and therefore knew the exact dimensions of the earth.[29]

The Great Pyramid is situated exactly on the 31°9' meridian east of Greenwich, and on the 29°58' 51" North Latitude.

This location is extremely significant as these meridians if extended exactly divided the land masses of earth into equal areas!

The pyramid is aligned within 4 minutes of a degree of the polar axis or True North.

This alignment is exceedingly sharp as the best modern science can do is the Paris Observatory which is 6 minutes of a degree off True North.

It is my belief that the pyramid was exactly on true north and the great earthquake of the 13th century shifted it slightly.

I also believe as a result of further research to be described later, that the earth's true and magnetic north poles were exactly aligned at that time.

The casing stones of the pyramid were cut and fitted with such precision that the joints, each with an area averaging 35 square feet, are no thicker than 0.001 inches, yet between each one is a thin film of cement.

Modern chemists have analyzed the cement but have

been unable to compound one of such fineness and tenacity as the cement in the Great Pyramid.

It is obvious from the above information that the Great Pyramid of Gizeh was built by minds of great genius, and constructed by a means we can not conceive.

The great building obviously was not built by a barbarian race for the purpose of housing mummies.

In fact the barbarian race that built the pyramid would have to have had a knowledge of mathematics only attributed to Pythagoras some several thousand years after the pyramid was supposed to have been constructed.

Chapter 6

PYRAMID RESEARCH PROJECTS

As a result of preliminary research, I began a series of serious research projects on the pyramid itself.

The following is a list of pyramids in tabular form:

Face Dimensions		*Pyramid*
BASE	SIDE	HEIGHT APPROX.
6″	5.7″	3.8″
12″	11.4″	7.6″
24″	22.8″	15.3″
36″	34.3″	22.9″
72″	68.5″	45.8″

The dimensions are based on the exact dimensions of the Pyramid of Gizch.

These are some of the dimensions of pyramids used in my experimental work.

Based on the fact that the Pyramid of Gizeh is the only pyramid in the world that is ventilated, I have also experimented with pyramids with windows in the sides.

The windows are holes up to 1/3 of the base length in diameter.

The holes do not detract from the function and seem to actually aid the processes going on inside the structure.

The pyramids were made of various materials including cardboard, wood, plaster, plexiglass, steel, copper, aluminum, cement and combinations of the above materials.

The materials used did not affect the results very much, however the size and orientation was of primary importance.

I at first believed the pyramid to work best when it was aligned to true north, however, after very careful research, I discovered the best alignment to be magnetic north, contrary to the alignment of the Great Pyramid.

This leads me to believe the Great Pyramid was built at a time when the earth's field was aligned to the polar axis.

It is not unusual for the poles to shift.

At the time of the writing of this paper, the earth's magnetic poles are shifting at a rate of 17 feet per month.[30]

In the duplication of Bovis' experiments, many perishable food items were tried in the pyramids of various shapes and sizes, of different materials, and different orientations, and in different locations in the pyramid itself.

The results of these experiments indicate that the best alignment is according to the magnetic axis.

An experiment to determine the validity of this theory was performed by the use of an external permanent magnetic field.

This is illustrated on Figure XVI.

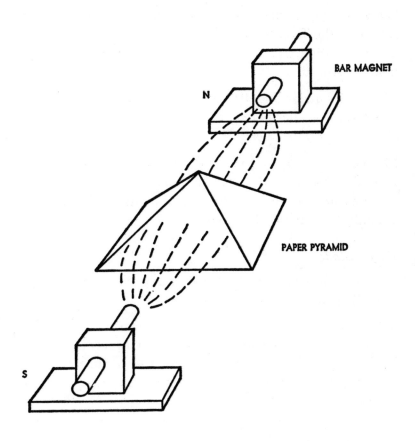

BAR MAGNET

N

PAPER PYRAMID

S

FIGURE XVI

Testing the effects of external magnetic fields on the pyramid.

The pyramid was a six inch base cardboard one.

The magnets are 5 inch alnico, the fields are on the order of 300 Gauss.

With the system described, I was able to get mummification of the foodstuffs with ANY alignment of the set, as long as the pyramid itself was aligned to the magnetic fields as shown.

The tables regarding the various food experiments are given in my earlier paper, *The Pyramid and Its Relationship to Biocosmic Energy*.[31]

My contribution to the field in food mummification is in the discovery that the pyramid will preserve food in any part of the structure as well as in the King's Chamber as reported by Bovis.

Razor Blades

In the duplication of Drbal's razor blade sharpener, the following discoveries were made:

Whereas Drbal theorized the crystal structure of the blade reformed, I believe the pyramid prevents a dulling effect due to contamination of the surface by skin oils and acids as well as the chemicals in shaving creams and soaps.

I shaved over 200 times with the blade treated in the pyramid. I also shaved an equal number of times with another blade by rinsing my razor out in pure de-ionized distilled water after every shave.

My razors normally go bad in three or four shaves.

There may also be a sharpening effect of a sort by the action of energy discharge from the sharp edges of the blade.

66

It is well known that any sharp object charged with any energy, whether magnetic, electromagnetic, or electric tends to concentrate and discharge from sharp surfaces and points when placed in a charged system.

From this point on, the experiments to be described are entirely the results of my own discoveries in the field.

Effects of Pyramid Energy on Living Organisms

The effects on the pyramid were tested on plants and human subjects.

Measurement of changes in the organism were made by means of Kirlian photography, GSR measurements of acupuncture points, Alpha wave detectors, and subjective responses.

Kirlian Measurements

The Kirlian photography set up is the same as illustrated in Figure IV.

The basic circuit of the oscillator is shown in Figure XVII.

The unit is a high frequency high voltage oscillator operating at 2 megahertz.

The oscillator voltage is continuously adjustable from zero to one hundred kilovolts by varying the spark gap over a limited range.

A timer is included in the primary line of the transformer to obtain precise exposures.

In practice, the unit is adjusted in a dark room so there

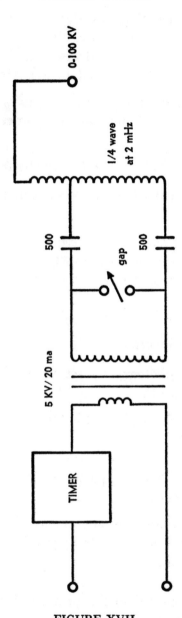

FIGURE XVII

High frequency high voltage oscillator for Kirlian photography.

is no visible corona discharge from the object to be photographed.

The only energy remaining is invisible ultra-violet light. Almost any film may be used with the system from Kodacolor to Polaroid.

This unit is a valuable tool for the study of the energy fields around living things.

Several hundred photographs were made of fingerprints and leaves before and after treatment with the pyramid.

Photographs were taken in both color and black and white.

The color photographs are particularly striking as they show changes in color as well as changes in brilliance and bioplasmic structure.

Figures XVIII and XIX are typical examples of photographs obtained with this technique.

Figure XVIII is composed of photographs of a man's fingerprint before and after treatment with the pyramid. The voltage setting and timing of the print remain the same.

The subject was placed in a simple 6 foot base vinyl plastic pyramid properly aligned to the magnetic poles.

The treatment of the subject was for ONE MINUTE in the pyramid.

The effect of the pyramid varies. It sometimes takes as long as half an hour in the unit to obtain similar results.

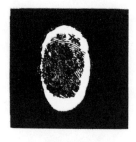 

BEFORE   AFTER

FIGURE XVIII

Kirlian photographs of same finger one minute apart. Before and after pyramid treatment.

BEFORE   AFTER

FIGURE XIX

Kirlian photographs of the same leaf, five minutes apart, before and after treatment in pyramids.

70

The aura or band of energy around the finger is rounder and larger than the aura in the first photo.

The fact that the energy content of the picture is larger and the shape is more rounded indicated an increase in aura without any loss of energy.

A more dramatic effect was obtained with a geranium leaf as illustrated in Figure IX.

The leaf had been off the plant for half an hour when the first photo was taken.

The energy field was almost completely gone as the leaf was dying.

In the next photograph the aura has increased considerably showing the recovery from only five minutes treatment in a small six inch base pyramid made of cardboard, again properly aligned to the magnetic poles.

The best results were obtained when the pyramids were set up outside the building.

The reason for this will be described in the next section on theory.

In the second photo, the leaf is filled to the brim, and many of the black spots are now filled with light.

The Kirlian technique can be used to obtain an ininstant measure of the result of various energy techniques such as Yoga breathing, meditation, and the effects of foods such as natural vs chemically grown, alcohol vs Ginseng, ozone vs oxygen, etc.

GSR Effects

Figure VIII is an example of a sensitive electronic

71

bridge for measuring minute as well as gross changes in GSR or galvanic skin resistance in living organisms.

The unit is extremely versatile as it can be balanced for measurement over a very wide range of input values.

The unit may be coupled to a recording oscillograph, or other means for permanent records of results.

The sensitivity can be adjusted to detect minute changes in resistance.

The normal electrode arrangement for plants is by means of German Silver electrodes.
The electrode arrangement is illustrated in Figure XX.

The electrodes should be cleaned with emery paper before every use.

The plant leaf should be free of dust.
The electrodes may be held in place by means of alligator clips.

The stand and flexible wire arrangement are necessary to prevent stress on the leaf.

Liquid electrodes have been tried, but I prefer the arrangement illustrated.

Small probe type electrodes have been tried with some gratifying results, but these have to be tested some more before these results are released.

The theory of using the small electrodes is to trace the plant's acupuncture points.

The plants exhibit many differing characteristics of change, they appear to sleep at times, and are very active at other times.

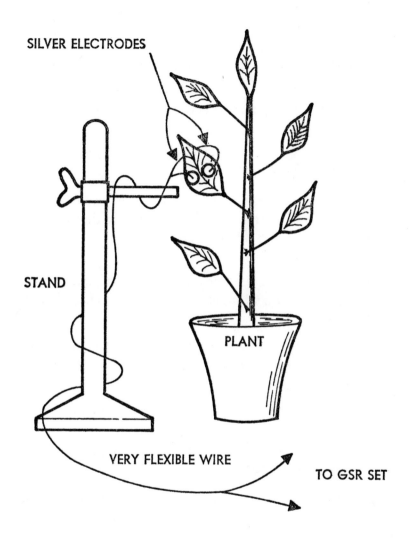

SILVER ELECTRODES

STAND

PLANT

VERY FLEXIBLE WIRE

TO GSR SET

FIGURE XX

Typical arrangement for measuring effect of pyramid on GSR of plants.

The main results are recognized as a very rapid change of resistance, a lowering, when a pyramid is placed over the plant.

Clear plexiglass pyramids as well as opaque cardboard ones have been used in the experiments.

The instantaneous changes occur under any type of pyramid.

An attempt to correlate change in resistance with strength of energy is somewhat successful.

There are no changes when the plant is sleeping.
It is easy to tell when a plant is sleeping by the response of the meter.

When the plant is responsive, there is a relaxation rate of change that is a continuous slow, sometimes fast change of resistance.

Changes in the environment, another person coming into the room, a change in color of illumination, a loud noise, all affect the plant.

Even the thoughts of the researcher have effects.

At times, the plant appeared to be oscillating with the heartbeat of the investigator.

At this time, when the signals are active, the plant will respond instantaneously to the effect of the pyramid.

Controls were made by lowering a plexiglass cube over the plant.

In the case of the equal volume cube, no changes were observed as they were with the pyramid.

Human GSR Measurements

The measurements on the body of a person are much more active than the ones measured with the plants.

The electrodes and arrangements have been described earlier.

The semiconductor effect, change of resistance with polarity of measurement from one side of the body to the other were measured, as well as basic changes in the normal resistance of the points in one direction.

In all cases with both male and female subjects, very rapid changes in GSR between acupuncture points occurred in all subjects.

Typical changes in less than five minutes of treatment were a balancing of the semiconductor effect, and a general lowering of resistance in the body.

Resistances as great as 150,000 ohms changed in less than five minutes to 2500 ohms.

The treatment pyramids were both the large 6 foot base and the small 6 *inch* base pyramids.

Tests were made on all areas of the body and the results all correlated: the pyramid caused an apparent balancing of the QI or TCH'I flows in the meridians.

The easiest points to measure are those on the head, and the semiconductor effect from hand to hand.

The exact points were located by means of the unidirectional electrode placement.

One electrode is placed on the earlobe, and the other is a small rounded test probe of the type used with multimeters.

The probe is run in the area of the point to be found until a gross change in resistance is found.

The exact spot is marked with a small washable marker pen.

The same procedure is then duplicated on the opposite side of the body for the corresponding opposite point.

At this time, two small electrodes are attached to the opposite points, and the points are measured from one to the other, changing the polarity of the electrodes and noting the resistance in both directions.

The differential is then noted.

With the electrodes attached, and the meter polarity adjusted to the polarity which gives the highest resistance, the pyramid is then lowered over the subject, or small pyramids are then placed over the points and adjusted to the magnetic poles.

The greatest changes were again noticed when the experiment was performed outside a building.

A very rapid decrease of resistance will be noted in the resistance of the point.

A change of polarity will show that the other side is also decreasing, but not as fast.

At some point, the resistance regardless of polarity will be the same or very close regardless of polarity.

The over all resistance of both points is often decreased considerably.

If the semiconductor effect is not observed on the first set of points, another meridian is chosen and measured until an unbalanced meridian is located.

The voltage and current from the GSR bridge is negligible, and has no effect on the points as the electro acupuncture described by the Chinese.

The balancing of semiconductor effect is observed after the subject is treated with the pyramid.

It should be stressed that the purpose of the experiments described is not to treat the subject with acupuncture, but to measure the pyramid's effect on the psychic energy points in the body.

The same results of GSR change were also noted with other developments such as the pyramid matrix and the pyramid energy plate to be described later.

Dielectric Constant of the Skin

Changes in skin dielectric constants were also measured on test subjects.

The test equipment is described in Figure VI.

A few of the electrodes are illustrated in Figure XXI.

The electrodes are three.

Coaxial, dual capacitor and single capacitor.

A constant pressure was applied to the head electrode arrangement by means of a constant tension band salvaged from an old pair of headphones.

The coaxial electrode is useful for measuring change in resonance or dielectric constant in a limited precise area.

The instrument used was a little more sophisticated.

77

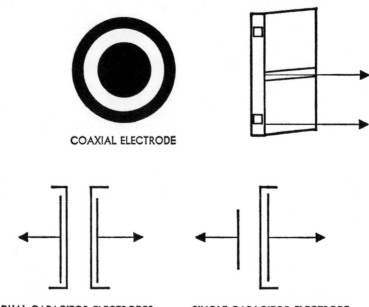

COAXIAL ELECTRODE

DUAL CAPACITOR ELECTRODES   SINGLE CAPACITOR ELECTRODE

CONSTANT PRESSURE HEADPHONE ADAPTER

FIGURE XXI

Typical electrode arrangement for measuring change in skin dielectric constant by resonance.

It was basically an oscillator consisting of the electrode arrangement as a frequency determining element.

The output of the oscillator is fed into a discriminator which simply converts the frequency changes into voltage change.

The voltage/frequency changes are then read directly on a zero centered volt meter.

The dual electrode arrangement is used for measuring the change across the whole body.

The single capacitor arrangement is coupled with a direct contact electrode and is used for tracing meridians over the skin surface.

The Capacitor in this arrangement is usually a very small disc or a small ball.

The dielectric or insulator used is 1/2 mil mylar tape placed over the surface of the capacitor.

The capacitors are conducting silver epoxy.

The electrode is made by turning a solid piece of acrylic stock in a lathe.

The side view of the coaxial electrode is an example.

The dark area is the sunken part of the block, the electrode area.

The wires are inserted in holes drilled from the other side.

The cavities are then filled with silver conducting epoxy.

The surface is then sanded smooth when the epoxy has set.

The electrode surface is polished with emery paper and

the dielectric covering is then placed on the surface of the electrode unit.

Alpha Rhythm Measurement

Much work needs to be done to correlate the results of the experiment to be described.

This experiment has been performed three times and needs to be done many more times to be conclusive.

One day while trying out an alpha feedback machine, one person was having a very hard time turning on alpha.

He would go through the various stages of relaxation and try as he may, he could not turn on alpha.

While his eyes were closed, I placed a 2 foot base pyramid over his head.

When the pyramid was lowered over his head, strong alpha came over the loudspeaker.

When the pyramid was removed, the alpha turned off.

When the test was repeated, the same results occurred.

The experiment has been duplicated on three people with the same results.

Subjective Reports

Several hundred people have sat in the 6 foot base plastic pyramids.

The tests were first run on friends who were asked to sit in the pyramid for half an hour and then asked to describe their feelings when they were in the structure.

The subjects were given no indication of what to expect.

In all cases, the subjects reported intense heat in the body and a tingling sensation in the hands.

The pyramid was then ventilated with large holes in the side as illustrated in Figure XII.

Even with large holes in the sides, they still reported an intense feeling of heat.

The description is similar to the Tibetan Tumo.

A number of people decided they wanted pyramids of their own.

My own body energy has increased since I began sleeping in the pyramid tent.

An effect reported by many is a sense of time distortion.

One subject sat in the pyramid for 4 hours and had the subjective impression that 1/2 hour had passed.

It had been stated by alpha researchers that a person in the alpha state loses all sense of time and space.[32]

This correlates with observed alpha activity in the pyramid

Meditation

Many of the subjects were interested in psychic phenomena and practice various forms of meditation.

ALL subjects who practice meditation have reported a significant increase in the effects of meditation in the pyramid.

81

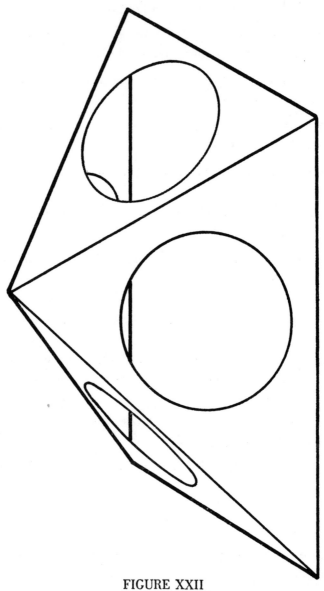

FIGURE XXII

Ventilated Pyramid Structure

Test results with the above structure indicated that holes as large as 1/3 the base length do not affect the properties of the pyramid.

82

This correlates with the theory that the Great Pyramid was built as a meditation chamber to develop psychic powers.

Animals

No extensive tests have been conducted on animals at this time.

There are however, three cases of interest.

A friend of mine placed his pet cat in a pyramid once a day for 1/2 hour.

The cat liked the pyramid and began to sleep in it.

When the test was begun, the cat had been a voracious meat eater.

After 6 weeks, the cat stopped eating meat and starved rather than eat meat.

Subsequent tests indicated that the cat had changed his diet and would only eat fruit and vegetables, cheese and nuts.

The animal became a vegetarian!

He ate raw vegetables and fruits of all descriptions; canteloupe, avocado, oranges, and watermelon.

The same thing happened to another cat as well as my own poodle.

Growth of Plants

A series of tests were run on the effects of pyramid treatments on the growth rate of plants.

The test plants were alfalfa sprouts.

I had some familiarity with sprouts as I had grown over 2500 pounds of them in the confines of my office!

The sprouts were treated three different ways: 1. treatment of feed water; 2. direct treatment of the plant in the pyramid; 3. treatment of the seed in the pyramid.

In all cases, identical tests were made in an identical volume cubic box as a control structure.

In all cases, the pyramid treated plants grew 2 to 3 times as fast as the controls, were more healthy and lasted longer after harvest.

One California grape farmer used my system on his irrigation system and his grape yield was 2-1/2 times the average yield of his neighbors and the California average.

Water Treatment

The water may be treated in several ways.
It may be placed in the pyramid in a container for a period of time depending on the size of the pyramid and the amount of water treated.

I used a 2 foot base pyramid and treated a quart bottle for 1/2 hour.

Another technique is to run water into a spiral coil placed in the pyramid and fashioned into a form of fountain.

Direct Treatment of Sprouts

The pyramid used was a one foot base unit made of clear plexiglass.

Four inch holes were cut in the sides for full ventilation.

The sprouts were grown entirely in the pyramid.

The controls were grown entirely in a well ventilated equal volume cube.

Treatment of Seeds

The seeds were placed in a 6 inch base cardboard pyramid for 8 hours.

Results

The water and plant treatments were best, the seed treatment was last.

The pyramid grown sprouts lasted over a week without spoilage after harvesting.

The controls on the other hand lasted 24 to 36 hours before spoilage.

Dehydration

Because of the dehydration or mummification of foods in the pyramid, I tried a number of experiments to see if the dehydration rate is accelerated in the pyramid.

It is not.

Normal dehydration occurs, the difference being that items placed in the pyramid do not decay while dehydrating.

Sprouts grown in the pyramid and left without water 24 hours do not die and decay as the controls do.

The controls developed odor and died.

The sprouts in the pyramid dehydrated slightly but did not decay and resumed normal growth when watering was resumed.

Short Term Effects On Foods, Change of Taste

During my original tests on mummification of foods, I used to taste the foods being treated to make sure they were really good.

Although there was no sign of decay, I wanted to see how the food tasted as it was undergoing the process of mummification.

I was in for a great surprise!

Not only did the foods taste good, they tasted better than they did before they were placed in the structure!

I began experimenting in earnest, and discovered that the pyramid could have an effect on the taste of food even when the food was treated for a surprisingly short duration.

I was so impressed by this new discovery that I began a series of double blind tests on the change of taste in foods.

I used several dozen people, and the test was conducted as follows:

The foods were all taken from the same source, that is the foods tested were the same food divided in half so the control would be the same as the treated sample except for the treatment.

The samples were then placed in paper cups with numbers on the bottoms.

The cups were then divided and recorded in a master file.

The ones chosen for the pyramid were then treated for five minutes in the pyramid.

The pyramid used for the tests was the 6 inch base ventilated.

The cups of food were then all mixed at random so no one knew which food was which.

Taste tests were conducted and 40 out of 48 people chose the foods treated in the pyramid as being more to their liking.

I like hundred percent results, so I interviewed the ones who missed on some of the foods and learned they were either heavy smokers or drinkers.

Subsequent interviews with a licensed wine taster confirmed my suspicions that people with certain eating and drinking habits cannot distinguish taste very well.

The foods tested were of all types; sweet, sour, various alcohols, fruits, and tobaccos.

Bitter and sour foods lose their bite, they become milder.

Sweet foods become sweeter.

Coffee loses its bitterness and tastes as if it were acid free.

Fruits increase in their qualities.

Acid tasting pineapple loses its acid taste and becomes as sweet as fresh ripe pineapple picked right out of the field.

Tobacco loses its harshness: Mexican black tobacco loses its harshness and tastes like mild choice Virginia.

The most dramatic effects occurred on pipe tobacco, unfiltered cigarettes, and cigars.

One of my associates smokes a very harsh unfiltered brand and uses a crystal type filter cigarette holder.

When his cigarettes were treated in the pyramid, he noticed he did not have to change his filter crystal so often.

Instead of changing it between every pack, he now has to change it after every three or four packs.

People who had whole cartons of their brands treated with the pyramid came back wanting their new cigarettes treated because they could not stand the harsh taste of their normal brand after smoking pyramid treated cigarettes.

Bananas and other perishables keep longer if they are treated in the pyramid for half an hour after they are purchased.

Controls all turned bad in a short time, and the fruits treated in the pyramids kept fresh up to twice as long as the controls.

Cut flowers take longer to die if they are placed in pyramid treated water.

Speaking of water, tests were run on the taste of regular city water treated in the pyramid.

The water used to water the plants.

All people who made the tests noticed the pyramid water tasted fresher and had less of a chemical or chlorine taste than the water which was untreated.

Other Pyramid Configurations

During the taste testing experiments, it was discovered that there was another phenomenon.

This new discovery is extremely significant.

I mentioned earlier that in any energy system, energy tends to discharge from sharp points.

This new discovery is that the pyramid also has energy coming from all of its five points!

A very fast test of this is to take a cup of coffee and divide it into two cups.

Then set up a small, say 6 inch base pyramid and align it to the magnetic poles.

Place one of the cups on the top of the pyramid for a minute or so and taste the difference!

This test came about as a result of some unexplained phenomena.

Some researchers tried the mummification experiments and their controls also mummified without decay.

I soon discovered that the control was affected by energy radiation effects off the points of the pyramid.

If the control is placed too close to the pyramid it is affected also!

The results of these experiments led to the development of a new contribution to the subject.

This new device is illustrated in Figure XXIII.

This new device I call the pyramid matrix or grid.

The matrix has been made in small one inch base pyramids.

These pyramids must be precision machined as a small error will affect results.

89

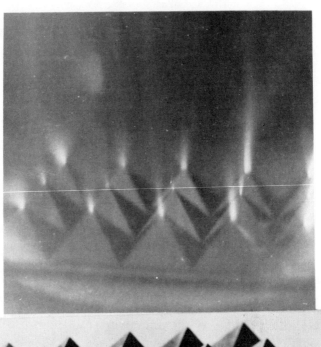

FIGURE XXIII

Pyramid grid or matrix uses radiation of energy from the points of the pyramid.

The matrix I have developed is a unit measuring 3 x 5 inches and has fifteen small pyramids on it.

Food placed on the top of the matrix is affected in the same way that food is affected in the big pyramid!

The matrix has been used with success in all the previously described experiments.

It is considerably more compact than the larger bulky pyramid.

Pyramid Energy Plate

As this item is of a highly proprietary nature, I cannot reveal the exact technique for its manufacture as patent applications are pending on it as well as the pyramid matrix.

This new device is a result of these researches and is simply a small aluminum plate which has been electronically charged with "amplified" pyramid energy.

This small 1/8 inch thick plate does everything the pyramid does and is very compact.

It too has been tested in all the projects and creates the same effects as the large pyramid.

It is not a primary pyramid structure and loses its charge after a while.

Best estimates of loss are at 3 years.

The pyramid experimental energy plate is a type of psychotronic device on the order of the Pavlita generators.

Psychotronic Twirler

Figure XXIV is a drawing of a PK device similar in nature to Pavlita's devices.

91

CUT SOLID LINES — FOLD DASHED LINES

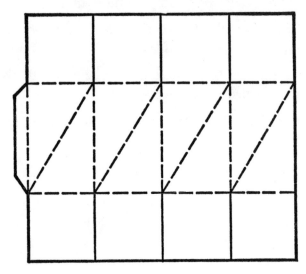

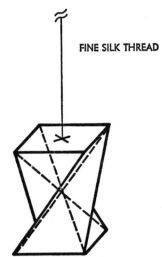

FINE SILK THREAD

PYRAMID PSYCHOTRONIC GENERATOR

FIGURE XXIV

Psychotronic Twirler.

This device is laid out in a pattern so anyone can construct it.

The solid lines are cut with scissors and the dotted lines are creased and folded.

A little experimentation will result in the suspended unit on the bottom of the page.

The device is suspended from a support by a very fine silk thread.

It may be enclosed in a glass tube to eliminate the effects of air currents.

The psychotronic twirler is basically two pyramids placed top to top . . . the proportions are the same as the Great Pyramid.

The use of the device is as follows:
The device is suspended and allowed to settle —so that it is not moving.

In order to start rotation, stare at the device with an intense gaze and concentrate entirely on it and its movement.

It will help to draw a zig zag figure on the surfaces of the pyramids to aid in the operation.

Follow the zig zags with the eyes.

After a bit of practice the device will spin and gain in velocity!

Another way of operating the device is as follows:

Operation of Twirler by TCH'I

Stand erect with the arms extended in front of the body.

While breathing deeply and rhythmically, open and close the hands rapidly many times; do this until the arms start to get tired.

The longer it is done, the more intense the effects.

When the arms are tired, hold the hands a few inches apart with the palms facing, and a strong flow of tingling energy will be felt.

This is the same as TCH'I or TUMO and KUNDALINI.

Hold the hands near the twirler and it will take off as the energy from the body enerigzes it.

Chapter 7

MEASURING DEVICES

There are two ways of measuring the relative values of energy in the vital energy systems.

The two systems are direct technical measurement, and the pseudo-technical or parapsychic system.

The first system is based on the repulsions and attractions as almost exclusively resorted to for measurement of physical phenomena. The balance measures the attraction exercised on bodies by the earth, the galvanometer measures the attraction exercised on a magnet by an electric current, the thermometer the attractions or repulsions of the molecules of a liquid submitted to the influence of heat.

The osmotic equilibria which control most of the phenomena of life are revealed by the attractions and repulsions of the molecules in the bosom of liquids.

The movements of various substances and the varieties of equilibrium resulting therefrom thus play a fundamental role in the production of phenomena.

They constitute their essence, and form the only realities accessible to us.

The technical measuring equipments used by the author in the preliminary researches have been described in the

sections on KIRLIAN PHOTOGRAPHY, GSR, DI-
ELECTRIC CONSTANTS, ELECTRIC FIELDS, etc.

There are others which are proprietary at this time.

Pseudo-technical and Parapsychic

There are many pseudo-technical or parapsychic instruments in use throughout the world.

I do not validate their use as scientific instruments, however I do recommend them for use in a pseudo-scientific
manner.

These devices have been in use for hundreds of years,
the most common form is the dowsing rod or water
witch used successfully in the search for water and
minerals.

My own experience in these devices is rather interesting as I was present at tests run at the Aberdeen Prov-
ing Ground for the use of such devices to find enemy tun-
nels in Viet Nam, and I understand these devices are in
use at this time to locate various enemy hiding places.

These devices all have one thing in common as they
require a human detector/mind combination for a readout device and are thus subject to more human error than
purely technical systems.

The basic principle of the para-psychic system is illustrated in Figure XXV.

This is the most sophisticated type of device, and has four
basic parts.

One or more of these parts are eliminated in some systems, however the part which must remain is the operator
or human mind.

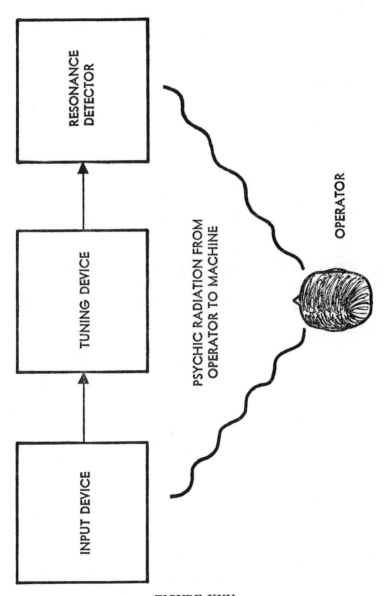

FIGURE XXV

Block Diagram of a para-psychic detector.

The Hieronymus Machine

On September 27, 1949, Thomas G. Hieronymus received patent number 2,482,773 for the *Detection of Emanations From Materials and Measurement of the Volumes Thereof.*

This is a milestone as it is the first patent ever issued on a psychotronic device.

A simplified block diagram of his machine is illustrated in Figure XXVI.

Because of the nature of his machine, and the desire to patent the basic device, he put a small amount of his total knowledge on the subject into his patent.

The patent basically describes a device for the detection of emanations from the basic elements, and is described as a machine for the analysis of minerals.

He has used it for far more things as described in his paper *Tracking the Astronauts in Apollo* 11.[33]

The basic principles of the machine are the three principles previously illustrated in Figure XXV.

The input part of the device may be any number of combinations, the one used by Hieronymus is a coil found around a plastic cup in which the sample to be analysed is placed.

Another type of input is a plastic plate with a spiral coil wound under it.

This device receives the emanations from the sample.

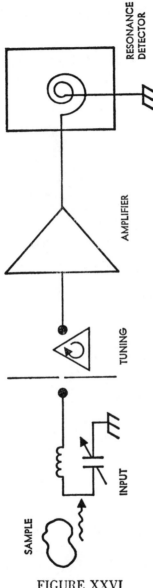

FIGURE XXVI

Hieronymus machine.

99

Tuning

In the case of the Hieronymus Machine, the tuning section is an optical slit which is fed into a prism.

Figure XXVII illustrates the optical slit and prism in better detail.

An alternative tuner is shown in Figure XXVIII.

It is said that these radiations which T. G. Hieronymus calls eloptic radiation follow the same laws as light.

The prism is rotated on a vernier dial, so the exact angle at which the prism is rotated may be duplicated.

A detector element, a small wire, intercepts the signal from the prism and the signal is amplified by an ordinary vacuum tube audio amplifier.

Resonance Detection

When the operator's mind and the emanations from the tuner arc on the same "wavelength" a type of resonance is established, and the detector indicates this mode.

The Hieronymus detector is simply a sheet of bakelite or plexiglass under which is placed a flat spirally wound coil, connected to the output of the amplifier and ground.

When resonance is established, there is a change of tactile characteristic in the top of the detector.

The change of characteristic is detected by lightly rubbing the fingertips on the surface of the detector plate while tuning the vernier dial of the prism.

When resonance is established, by the position of the vernier dial, and the thought held by the mind of the

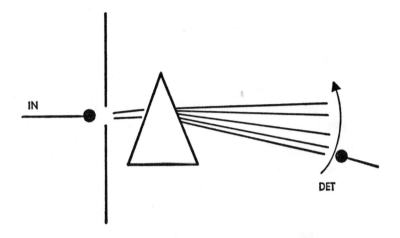

FIGURE XXVII

Prism Technique Rotate prism or detector element.

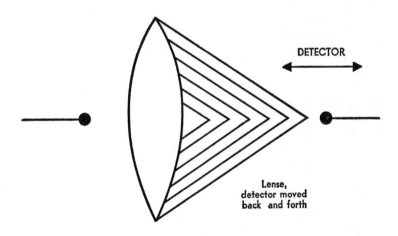

FIGURE XXVIII

Two means of separating frequencies of eloptic or biocosmic energy. These are methods employed by Hicronymus.

101

operator, a note is made of the prism angle as determined by the vernier scale.

Hieronymus has established numbers which correlate with the known chemical elements and combinations.

The thing which makes the system useful is that more than one operator can use the machine and obtain the same results!

Hieronymus has credentials to back up his claims; he is a Fellow of the American Institute of Electrical and Electronic Engineers, and is a Registered Professional Engineer.

Although the Hieronymus machine cannot be explained by modern physics, it does have merit by the fact that the results can be duplicated.

An old saying goes, "every progressive spirit is opposed by a thousand men appointed to guard the past."

In the past, whenever new inventions or discoveries became completely unaccountable to the orthodox men then in power, the great pioneers were imprisoned.

Men like Galileo were imprisoned, men like Giordano Bruno were burned at the stake.

In our own time, Professor Goddard, the father of modern rocketry was called "moon mad Goddard" by his fellow scientists.

T. G. Hieronymus is certainly a pioneer in this new field.

Various other input devices, tuners, and detectors can be substituted for the various parts of the basic psychotronic machine and the system will still work.

The detectors can be altered by the addition of microphones to detect the difference in tactile characteristics and to amplify these microsonic changes.

George DeLaWarr in England developed a machine he claimed to be a precise detector, he called it a radionic device.[34]

De LaWarr used a cavity input device, a ratio-tuner (to be described), and a hollow tactile box for the resonance detection.

Other researchers use a pendulum for detection of resonance. The author believes the pendulum to be the least reliable as it is the easiest device to "fool" by unconscious reflexes.

All these devices rely on the subconscious and on the mental training of the operator.

For these reasons, these devices are only as reliable as the operator.

In my research into these devices, I have developed a unit of my own as illustrated in Figure XXIX.

Flanagan Psychotronic Detector

The input of the machine is simply a flat spirally wound coil of insulated wire placed under a clear plexiglass sheet.

The output of the coil is fed into a potentiometer which is used as an attenuator to determine the strength of the emanation.

The tuning section is a series of 9 potentiometers arranged as illustrated.

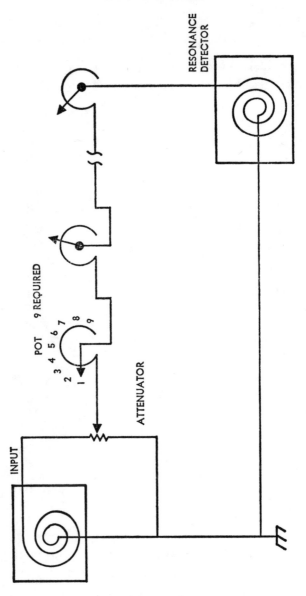

FIGURE XXIX
Ratio Psychotronic Detector.

These tuning devices are based on the idea that these radiations can be tuned by dividing a detector or tuning element into ratios which can be duplicated from machine to machine, thus every radiation will have a ratio of its own.

The output sensor or resonance detector is a coil, like the input, and is used to detect tactile changes in the plate.

The above machine is not meant to be a scientific device but is designed in the spirit of similar devices used by others in their own research.

The author has had some luck with the device, and it has given many hours of delight to others who have tried it.

Chapter 8

THEORY OF ENERGIES

The first part of this paper dealt with the presently known history of vital or life energies.

The basic problem was attacked from a purely philosophical pseudo-scientific viewpoint.

There are theories in the purely physical sciences that support the existence of other energies.

These theories have been discarded for the acceptance of purely mathematical models.

The author believes the existence of these energies was neglected because there has not been a satisfactory ETHER THEORY.

A mechanical ether theory is required to have a full understanding of the universe.

Following is an ether-vortex theory that does have workability.

A full understanding of the energies in the physical universe may be slow in coming without acceptance of such a theory.

The theory to be presented is not the product of one mind, it is the product of thousands of years of man's endeavoring to understand the mechanics of the universe.

The format of the following theory is in the author-year presentation, the references can be found in any good physics library.

106

It is often stated that the function of science is to make observations and measurements and to find correlations between the observed facts.

That such pursuits belong properly to the realm of science is not limited to purely empirical or inductive methods of investigation.

Any procedure by which the facts of nature can be ascertained or surmised or rendered more intelligible and less mysterious deserves to be recognized as a truly scientific pursuit.

Modern physics is devoted largely to the use of mathematical symbols and equations, but the success of this method does not justify us in condemning the use of geometric forms and models as unscientific.

Mechanical and hydromechanical models are based primarily on geometric or space relationships, and geometry, even solid geometry, is a branch of mathematics . . . a fact too often ignored by the exponents of the "new physics."

These considerations are especially pertinent in the field of atomic structure where geometric relationships must be presumed to be of primary importance although hidden from direct view and in many cases not easily expressed by mathematical equations.

Physicists may be correct in their assertions that nothing is truly scientific unless it can be expressed mathematically, but the author maintains that no system of atomic structure is truly scientific unless it can be expressed geometrically by pictures or diagrams . . . "structure" by its very definition being something that must have geometric form.

107

There has been much philosophical argument over whether the external world really exists, and whether the expression "physical reality" has any meaning.

If we adopt the idealistic view that matter does not exist as an objective reality but only as a product of the mind, then the primary purpose of theoretical physics should be to study the mental processes rather than physical phenomena so as to ascertain the clearest and most satisfactory symbolic representations of the facts of nature by means of mathematical formulas and equations.

This is exactly the attitude taken by the leading physicists of today, with the result that nearly all recent books on quantum mechanics and atomic structure are couched in such language that it is impossible to tell where the world of physical reality ends and where the world of mathematical fancy begins.

If we ask any exponent of "the new physics" whether the electrons actually move in orbits about the atoms, we will probably get a lesson in jesuitism for a reply, but never a direct answer of "yes" or "no".

On the other hand if we adopt the materialistic view of the general public that matter does exist of its own accord, then the primary purpose of theoretical physics should be to ascertain the true facts of nature, regardless of whether or not they will readily lend themselves to mathematical treatment.

For example, in the case of atomic structure, the Bohr atom with its planetary electrons travelling in a grooved ether will lend itself to mathematical treatment more readily than the new vortex atom with its complex system of circulating ether currents; but the latter is probably a closer approximation of what actually exists in nature.

This difficulty of expressing vortex structures mathematically was recognized by A. A. Michelson (1911, p. 162) when he wrote that:

"The mathematics of the subject is unfortunately very difficult, and this seems to be one of the principal reasons for the slow progress made in the theory."

The author takes the materialistic view for granted and will proceed with the assumption that the external world really exists.

The vortex atom structures herein presented purport to be at least approximately true representations of what actually exists in nature, and not merely convenient symbolic fictions.

This is more than can be conscientiously claimed for the Rutherford-Bohr atom.

Nature is psychical as well as physical, and during the process of evolution psychical development takes place simultaneously with physical development.

It could not be otherwise because the psychical is the subjective aspect of that of which the physical is the objective aspect, and the one is just as real as the other.

Both are attributes or apects of nature, and more specifically of the ether.

The Hydromechanical Ether

For several decades the physics profession has been contending that the hypothesis of an ether serves no other purpose than to supply a subject for the verb "to move" or "to undulate".

109

There are, however, many things in nature besides movements or undulations.

There are at least three elementary forces which act at a distance; gravitational, electric and magnetic forces, and at least three different subatomic particles; protons, electrons, and neutrons, of which all matter is composed.

The modern physics profession with its etherless universe has not yet given us a satisfactory explanation for a single one of these elementary forces or subatomic particles, but we do have such explanations under the new vortex theory which would have no meaning or significance and would never have been thought of without the assumption of an ether.

It may be true that the existence of an ether has never been proved within a strict meaning of the word "proof", but we do have an abundance of indirect evidence of its existence, and certainly its existence has never been disproved . . . not even by the Michelson-Morley (1881-1887) experiment.

On the contrary, the positive first-order results obtained in the Sagnac (1913) experiment, and also in the Michelson-Gale (1925) experiment, would be difficult to explain on any other basis.

If we were to deny the existence of an ether, then we would also have to deny the existence of the world because there could not be any world unless there exists some substance of which the world is composed.

Furthermore, the ether must be something which occupies space and is capable of moving so as to have fluidity which reduces it to a hydromechanical ether, but not necessarily to the completely frictionless and non-viscous ether of the 19th century.

The concept of a single primordial substance can be traced at least as far back as Anaximander (611-547 B.C.) whose "Infinite" corresponds in every respect to the present day concepts of the ether.

Anaximander was closely followed by Heraclitus (535-475 B.C.) whose "Fiery Ether" had the same general significance as the Infinite of Anaximander, but with a more dynamic aspect, thus resembling more closely the dynamic vortex ether which was later revived by Rene Descartes (1596-1650) in his theory of celestial vortices.

Soon thereafter, Johann Bernoulle (1667-1748) deduced Kepler's laws from Descartes' theory of vortices, but in the meantime, Isaac Newton (1642-1727) had introduced his mathematical theory of gravitation and his corpuscular theory of light, both of which were based on the assumption that free space was completely empty, and not filled with a dynamic ether, as assumed by Descartes.

Sometime later, Michael Faraday (1781-1867) made use of an elastic solid concept of the ether, after which James Clerk Maxwell (1831-1897) revived the ether vortex theory in the field of electromagnetism, and George Stokes (1819-1903) then sponsored a dynamic ether concept which could have been easily reconciled with the ether vortex concept of Descartes.

In the opposite direction, and in line with the Newtonian empty space idea, was the stagnant ether theory of H. A. Lorentz (1853-1928), a close forerunner of the Poincare-Einstein theory of relativity.

111

The Michelson-Morley experiment in 1881, however, proved that the Lorentz theory of a quiescent stationary ether was wrong.

A choice then had to be made between a dynamic intersteller ether as conceived by Descartes and Stokes, or merely empty space without any ether, as conceived by Newton and Einstein.

The Einsteinians have prevailed thus far, and are still in the majority, but the question is still being argued, and is by no means settled.

Many who profess to seek knowledge ignore the most significant features that nature displays, and prefer to seek knowledge in almost any place but where it is to be found.

The ether with which the twentieth century vortex theory deals, is a new type of hydromechanical ether, which does not contain any atomic oscillators, and is therefore free from ordinary frictional viscosity; but which does have a sort of idealized or quasi-frictional viscosity by virtue of which its direction of flow is controlled, without any dissipation of energy.

A body which is moving through such a fluid will continue to move at constant velocity in accordance with Newton's first law of motion.

Any portion of the fluid which is in its path will be deflected around it so as to form an enveloping vortex that moves along with the body (see Hilgenberg, 1939).

If the fluid has mass and inertia, as presumably every fluid must have, then such a moving body would have to do work upon the fluid ahead of it, to push it out of the way; but the deflected fluid, after bypassing the body, will immediately return its kinetic energy to the rear side of the same body.

A portion of the kinetic energy of the moving body, will, therefore, be contained in the fluid vortex which moves along with the body, but the total kinetic energy of the moving system, will remain the same.

This is exactly the behavior that would be required of an interplanetary ether which permits the planets to move freely through it, but which is also carried along locally by the moving planets, so that there will be no observable ether drift along the surface of any planet, except that which is due to the rotation of the planet on its axis.

Such a quasi-frictional concept of the ether may have been inherent in Descartes' theory of vortices, but its importance was not fully appreciated until the early part of the 20th century, when it was vigorously sponsored by Hermann Fricke of Germany, at about the time when Poincare and Einstein introduced the special theory of relativity.

It has the advantage over special relativity in that it represents a system which can be visualized, whereas special relativity cannot be visualized, but can only be expressed mathematically.

Special relativity is therefore only a mathematical evasion, and not an explanation.

The failure of physicists to recognize that there can be a quasi-frictional viscosity without any thermal dissipation of energy, has been one of the most serious mistakes which they have made during modern times.

Such a concept is not self-contradictory, but can be illustrated by a fish gliding through the water under its own inertia; the frictional dissipation of energy in such a case being negligible.

It is also illustrated by the flow of electrons along a superconductor, at a temperature near absolute zero, where the atomic oscillators have settled down to such a degree of quiescence that they are no longer aroused to activity by the migration of the electrons.

A purely hydromechanical interpretation of the ether is generally thought to be inadequate to account for the elementary particles of matter with their associated fields of force; or for light waves with transverse displacement, but as long as we have not yet made any exhaustive study of frictionless hydromechanics, we are not justified in summarily rejecting such a concept as inadequate.

The presence of a transverse displacement in light waves does not necessarily preclude the possibility of a longitudinal displacement.

The transverse displacement may have been accentuated at the expense of the longitudinal displacement by passage through the polarizing apparatus.

It has been shown by R. Wussow (1928) that such a transformation is conceivable, but if light waves do have such a longitudinal displacement, then the ether would have to be accredited with at least a limited compressibility.

An infinitely compressible ether is so difficult to form any clear concept of, that it may be left out of consideration.

114

It is doubtful whether light waves could travel with a finite velocity in an infinitely compressible ether, and a vortex motion could not therein exist.

The ether must be either entirely incompressible, or must have only a limited compressibility.

Since our experience with material systems has taught us that compressional elasticity is always associated with bodies consisting of discrete elementary particles, it seems that a primordial substrate like the ether, which presumably does not have any atomic constitution, could also not have compressibility.

In the absence of any atomic oscillators, an incompressible ether with any viscosity at all, and especially with an INERTIAL viscosity of the type hereinafter described, should be capable of transmitting waves with transverse displacement.

Such waves, when they occur in a fluid medium, are generally referred to as electromagnetic, rather than hydromechanical, but as will be explained in detail later, electromagnetism can itself be reduced to a hydromechanical basis.

The term "viscosity" has been used hereinabove with reference to the ether so as to conform to the terminology which is now in general use; but in the physics literature of today, this term is usually applied to material fluids which have internal friction and are capable of thermal dissipation of energy.

For describing a frictionless fluid like the ether, we should use a term with broader meaning, so as to be applicable to the idealized viscosity of the ether, in which the resistance to motion is not caused by internal friction due to the presence of atomic oscillators, but by IN-ERTIAL reaction of the surrounding fluid.

The term VISCIDITY seems to meet this requirement, and will henceforth be used instead of viscosity in referring to the ether.

The viscidity of the ether is not frictional viscidity resulting from any complex internal structure of the ether, but is inertial viscidity such as is necessarily present in any fluid which is capable of moving, and a fluid which is not capable of moving is inconceivable.

Since inertia itself is therefore merely an aspect of motion, it necessarily follows that a viscidity of the kind that exists in the ether is merely an aspect of motion.

It is due to the inertial continuity of the motion itself, and, without such inertial continuity there could not be any motion at all.

The 19th century ether which did not have any viscidity, was, therefore, a theoretical impossibility.

An ether with viscidity is the only kind of an ether that is conceivable.

Although the density of the ether, according to O. C. Hilgenberg, is only about 0.027 milligram per cubic centimeter, it must have a very high viscidity in order to transmit waves with the velocity of light.

If an ordinary liquid consisting of atoms, or molecules, would have a proportionately high viscosity, then the internal frictional losses would be too great to permit any effective propagation of waves; but if the ether has any internal friction at all, then such a friction must be so slight as to be noticeable only as the red shift of the spectra of distant nebulae.

Certainly the ether does not have any atomic oscillators in it, and would therefore be incapable of any dissipation of energy in the form of heat.

Any work that is done upon any portion of the ether could be spent only in overcoming the inertia of that portion.

No matter how great its viscidity may be, there would still be complete fluidity.

High viscidity, and complete fluidity, are not contradictory or mutually exclusive properties, since complete fluidity requires that there must not be any internal friction; either static or dynamic whereas high viscidity of the kind that exists in the ether, requires only that internal displacements be propagated laterally, and such lateral propagation does not depend on frictional dissipation of energy.

The hydromechanical concept of the ether is not as contradictory as some of the substitutes that have been offered for it.

As for example, Einstein's second postulate of relativity. All electric and magnetic action at a distance is proof of the internal viscidity of the ether, and such viscidity is easier to visualize than light waves whose velocity, relative to the observer, remains the same; regardless of whether the observer is moving toward or away from, the approaching waves.

Before we reject the concept of a hydromechanical ether as inadequate, we should also give consideration to the fact that we know only very little about the motion of fluids where sources and sinks are present, which includes vortex motion; every vortex ring having associated with it a source on one side, and a sink on the other side.

In ordinary liquids and gasses, such vortex motion rapidly disappears because of internal friction, but in an ether that does not have in it, any atomic oscillators, and therefore no internal friction, such vortex motion and the sources and sinks associated therewith, would be perpetual, regardless of how great its viscidity may be.

A high degree of viscidity may have its effect on the forms and dimensions of the vortices, but would not cause their destruction, or prevent their existence if the viscidity is due to inertial reaction, and not to internal friction.

The opinion has been expressed by Einstein, and others, that the concept of motion, although applicable to all molecular and corpuscular fluids, is not applicable to a homogeneous and structureless fluid like the ether.

It seems however, that this objection is without merit, because the concept of motion is complete in itself, regardless of what it is that moves.

We should not form too materialistic a concept of the ether, because it is not a MATERIAL substance, but rather the common substrate of both matter and mind.

The concept of motion has a different meaning with respect to material substances, because a material substance remains in existence after OBSERVABLE motion has ceased, whereas the ether may be of such a nature that it depends for its very existence, on its motion.

Movement of the ether is a noumenon rather than a phenomenon, and therefore cannot be dealt with in the same manner as movement of a material substance.

An ether which is capable of moving would necessarily have inertia, because inertia, although usually referred to as a property of matter, is primarily a property of motion.

Inertia means nothing more than continuity of motion, and all motion necessarily has continuity as long as the motion continues.

If the motion is rotation, or movement in a closed circuit, as in the case of vortex motion, then the inertia will be localized, and localized inertia is just another name for momentum.

Hence, in order to account for the elementary particles of matter, we need only to have an ether that is capable of moving.

Today, the hydromechanical type of ether is generally thought to be inadequate to account for the behavior of light waves under the relativity and quantum theories.

Thus, according to the special relativity theory of Poincare and Einstein, which should not be confused with Newtonian or classical relativity, light waves are always supposed to travel with the same velocity relative to the observer, regardless whether he is moving toward or away from the approaching waves, and, according to the usual interpretation of the quantum theory, such waves are also supposed to remain segregated in separate bundles or "photons" instead of spreading out in all directions like sound waves.

119

We must, however, distinguish between the observed facts themselves, and some of the startling theories that have been introduced by physicists of the Einstein-Planck school.

The special relativity theory was offered primarily as an explanation for the Michelson-Morley experiment which has heretofore always been performed with the interferometer arranged horizontally so as to rotate about a vertical axis.

Such an apparatus would respond to horizontal ether currents only, and since all horizontal directions are physically equivalent, the results have always been negative, as might have been expected.

The apparatus was not sensitive enough to detect the slight horizontal drift of the ether, due to the rotation of the earth on its axis.

As suggested by O. C. Hilgenberg (1939), the experiment should have had the interferometer arranged in a vertical plane, so as to rotate about a horizontal axis, it being only in the direction of the dominant gravitational forces where any substantial movement of the ether could possibly occur; but even in the vertical direction, we should hardly expect any deviation from the normal velocity of light, because, otherwise, the North Star, as viewed at different hours during the night, would appear to be going around in a circle.

If the force of gravity is due to an inward drift of the ether, then it is probably accompanied by a simultaneous outward migration of high velocity jets, as will be explained later, and these two movements probably cancel each other out, in their effect upon light radiation.

120

The negative result of the Michelson-Morley experiment seems to have been correctly explained by George Stokes, who considered the ether as being carried along by the earth's gravitation field; however, the relativists insisted that Stokes' theory was contradicted by astronomical aberration, and those who were of a different opinion were simply not given a chance to be heard.

For instance, the German physicist, L. Zehnder, after two unsuccessful attempts to get the German Physical Society to publish his article on Stokes' theory and aberration, finally had to content himself with getting it published in the ASTRONOMISCHEN NACHRICHTEN, where it has remained hidden and buried in the dust ever since.

Other physicists with similar views have been less successful than Zehnder, and had to depend on privately published monographs for an expression and recording of their views.

If there has been anybody who was really competent to say whether the Michelson-Morley experiment has disproved the existence of an ether, it was A. A. Michelson himself; and Michelson has always been an ardent advocate, not only of the ether vortex theory, but also of Stokes' concept of the ether.

Stokes' theory was later corroborated by both the Sagnac experiment in 1913, and the Michelson-Gale experiment in 1925.

Although these two experiments have clearly disproved the Poincare-Einstein theory of relativity, the physics textbooks of today are still confidently expounding Ein-

121

stein's theory, without ever mentioning the experiments by which that theory has been disproved.

In the Sagnac experiment, two simultaneously emitted light signals were sent in opposite directions around a closed path, and a photographic plate was arranged to record the interference fringes at the place where the signals met.

The entire apparatus was supported on a turntable.

The results showed that when the table was slowly rotated, it took one of the light signals a longer time, and the other one a shorter time, to reach their final meeting place than when the turntable was not rotated.

Similar positive, first-order results were obtained in the Michelson-Gale experiment, which showed on a much larger scale that the velocity of light at the surface of the earth, is less in the direction of the earth's rotation, than in the opposite direction.

These experiments seem to show that the ether at the surface of the earth is carried along completely by the earth in its orbital movement about the sun, but that it does not partake of the rotation of the earth on its axis.

The reason why this rotational drift of the ether has not been detected in the Michelson-Morley experiment is because the effect is too small.

The earth moves in its orbit about the sun with a velocity of nearly 20 miles a second, whereas, the peripheral velocity which is due to the rotation of the earth is only about 1/3 of a mile per second at the equator, and less elsewhere.

Stokes' theory is also corroborated by the orbital movement of the planets about the sun, and the satellites about the planets.

The sun itself moves through interstellar space, relative to the fixed stars, with a velocity of 19.6 kilometers per second, while the planets move in nearly circular orbits about the sun.

The planet Jupiter, for example, moves along its orbit at a uniform velocity of 13 kilometers per second.

This is readily explainable if we assume that the ether in the neighborhood of Jupiter is carried along by Jupiter's gravitational field, and that Jupiter swims in this ether, like a fish in water.

How else could we possibly explain such uniform orbital movement in the absence of any ether?

If Jupiter obeys Newton's first law of motion, as presumably it must, and if there is no ether, then we could only assume that Jupiter moves along at a uniform velocity relative to the fixed stars.

Since, however, the sun moves along faster than Jupiter, it would be impossible for Jupiter ever to get to the other side of its orbit, unless we make the fantastic assumption that it is speeded up in one half of its orbit, and slowed down in the other half.

Newton's first law of motion would then have no meaning at all.

Obviously, the true system of reference in each case is then the ether, whose position is determined by the fixed stars for measuring the velocity of the sun, and by the gravitational field of the central body for measuring the orbital velocity of a planet or satellite.

The photon theory was introduced about half a century ago by Max Planck as a possible interpretation of his radiation formula, in an effort to explain the spectrum of black body radiation.

Planck's radiation formula is still being interpreted to mean that the radiant energy of light in free space does not spread out uniformly in all directions like sound waves, but remains segregated in separate bundles of "photons".

Since the atoms at the time when Planck developed his radiation formula were not considered as having definite structures, it is not surprising that the quantization of energy was attributed to the radiaticn itself, rather than the atomic oscillators by which such radiation was absorbed or emitted.

Today, however, we know that the atoms are highly organized structures which would be expected to radiate or absorb their energy in quantized amounts, and if such spontaneous quantization of energy is accomplished by the atoms themselves, then the photon theory becomes superfluous.

Since the quantization of energy is a function of the atom and not of the ether, it is not necessary to ascribe to the ether any complicated structure or any strange or mysterious behavior.

It can be considered as a simple hydromechanical fluid, devoid of all complications.

The existence of an ether is a logical necessity and does not involve any contradictions.

Since positive results have been obtained in all experiments where positive results could be expected, there is no justification for all the present-day uncertainty as to its existence.

Subatomic Vortices and the Three Elementary Forces

It is said that any theory which purports to tell us what electricity and the elementary particles of matter really are, stands condemned at the start.

Although it is true that we cannot make something out of nothing, still we do not need to begin with a complex array of protons, electrons, and neutrons as a starting point.

These subatomic particles, and their associated fields of force, may themselves consist of self sustaining forms of motion; such as vortex motion, in a hypothetical ether having only certain general properties, such as inertia and fluidity, but no specific internal structure or molecules with atomic oscillators.

Any fluid medium that is capable of supporting wave motion, should also be capable of supporting vortex motion, and it would seem inconsistent, after recognizing light as a wave motion in the ether, to refuse to recognize the elementary particles of matter as vortex motion in the same ether.

Nevertheless, in the modern physics literature, the word "vortex" has been about as taboo as the word *ether,* and for apparently no reason except emotional prejudice.

The physics profession has been inconsistent in maintaining an antagonistic attitude toward some hypotheses while swallowing others whole.

It cannot be said that the ether vortex concept is superfluous and of no value.

125

It has not only led to satisfactory explanations for many of the previously unexplained phenomena of physics and chemistry, but it has also provided us with a tangible concept to facilitate our thinking about otherwise abstract subjects.

The distinguishing characteristic of all elementary particles of matter is their LOCALIZED PERSISTENCE OF INDIVIDUALITY, and this is also the distinguishing characteristic of vortex motion.

Wave motion is not localized like the elementary particles of matter, nor does it have individuality within the full meaning of that term.

As an example, when a wave is distorted, it will not of its own accord revert to its original form, but will travel in the directions normal to the new wavefront; there being no persistence of individuality or memory of the original form of the wave.

On the other hand, if a vortex ring is distorted from the circular, into the elliptical form, it will spontaneously revert to the original circular form.

The vortex ring therefore does have persistence of individuality and memory of its original form.

Although it is true that a spring, or rubber band, will spontaneously revert to its original form, nevertheless, such spontaneous action of a resilient material body is not an explanation of its resiliency, but only an EXPRESSION thereof.

The behavior of a resilient material body is merely the combined action of its constituent atoms and molecules, and therefore depends on the resiliency of the materials of which it is made, whereas the resiliency of a vortex ring does not depend on the nature of its material, but is an inherent characteristic of the form of the motion itself.

A vortex ring will not only tend to maintain its circular form, but will also dynamically and resiliently maintain its dimensions and proportions.

There is obviously a lower limit to the possible overall diameter of the ring, because after the opening at the center is completely closed, the ring cannot become any smaller.

The inevitable crowding of the ether in the region of this central opening, will, however, prevent any such complete closure of the ring; but will tend to expand the ring to a larger over-all diameter.

In opposition to this expansive force, there are other forces acting in the radially inward direction, and tending to compress or contract the ring to a smaller diameter.

One of these inwardly acting forces is caused by the impacts of external ether currents against the outer periphery of the ring.

Another such force is caused by the centrifugal forces inside the rotating filament.

The immediate result of such centrifugal forces will be to make the filament thicker, but since its volume must remain constant, any thickening of the filament must be accompanied by an equivalent reduction of the overall ring diameter.

The ring will, therefore, not expand indefinitely, but will acquire and maintain definite size and proportions.

127

Physicists usually try to summarily dismiss the new vortex atom theory with the comment that it is merely the revival of the 19th century theory of Lord Kelvin, which proved to be a failure.

The broad concept of vortex atoms did not, however, originate with Kelvin, but can be traced at least as far back as 1674, when Nicolas Malebranche stated in his "Recherche de la Verite" that "la matiere subtile ou etheree est necessairement composee de petits turbillons".

Since the new vortex theory deals primarily with the vortex structures of the subatomic particles (protons, electrons, and neutrons), it obviously cannot be the same as Kelvin's theory since these subatomic particles were not known during the time of Kelvin.

These subatomic particles are very specific in their behaviors, and must be presumed to have specific structures, because it is a universal rule, without any exception, that specific behavior can be explained only on the basis of specific structure.

As long as no other type of structure has ever been suggested for these subatomic particles, we must proceed with the assumption that they have vortex structures.

The ether, according to Kelvin's theory, was not only frictionless, but also devoid of any viscidity, so that adjacent vortices could have no coordinating effect upon one another, whereas, in this new theory, the vortices are in a viscid, but non-frictional, ether, similar to that contemplated by Maxwell, Stokes, and Fricke.

In the Kelvin vortex rings, the velocity of circulation of the ether would presumably be proportional to the radial distance from the center of rotation, but would suddenly drop to zero at the surface of the ring, whereas, in the 20th century vortex rings, the velocity at the surface of the ring (assuming that it has a definite surface) does not drop suddenly to zero, but tapers off gradually in the outward direction.

This external circulation is directly involved in all physical and chemical activity, and when it becomes too crowded, the atom bursts to pieces with the liberation of much energy, as in the splitting of the uranium atom.

One of the objections which was raised against the 19th century vortex theory, was that a vortex ring in a frictionless ether, could never be started, but that if it ever did come into existence, then it could never be destroyed.

This would probably be true of the Kelvin vortex rings, but would not be true of the vortex rings in the new 20th century ether, or in any fluid which has even a slight degree of viscidity.

Any sudden impulse in such a liquid or fluid would be likely to form, at least temporarily, a vortex ring therein.

According to A. Betz (1950), such a vortex ring would be produced by the rolling up of a shear surface in the form of a cylindrical sheet.

Another effect of such viscidity is to cause adjacent vortex rings to exert a co-ordinating effect upon each other, so as to bring them into axial alignment and rolling contact whenever possible; which Kelvin's 19th century vortex rings in a non-viscid ether would not do.

If we assume that face-to-face rolling contact is a necessary and sufficient reason and condition for structural stability, then with two vortex rings, it will be possible to produce two different stable structures with the adjacent sides of the two rings moving either inwardly, or outwardly, but not in opposite directions.

These two structures will also have different external circulations; the one being the reverse, but not the equivalent of, the other.

This immediately suggests a much needed structural basis for protons and electrons, and for the electrical fields associated therewith.

The problem now is to determine which of these two structures is the proton, and which is the electron.

The proton differs from the electron in having greater mass, and therefore more internal energy, which means it is a more stable structure than the electron.

The greater mass of the proton cannot be satisfactorily explained by merely assuming that the vortex rings of the proton are larger than those of the electron, because we would then have difficulty in drawing a satisfactory picture of the neutron.

The cores or filaments of the two vortex rings themselves will undoubtedly contribute some to the mass of the proton, but if the ether has a density of only 0.027 milligrams per cubic centimeter, as calculated by O. C. Hilgenberg, then the inertial effect of the ether inside the core or filament would be too small to account for the actual mass of the proton.

An ether vortex ring always occupies two regions;

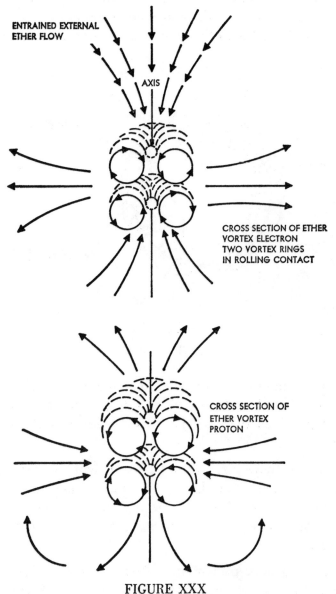

FIGURE XXX

Vortex Electron and Proton

namely, the rotating inner core of the ring, and the surrounding space in which the ether flows in paths that
are interlinked with the core, but not necessarily in closed
circuits.

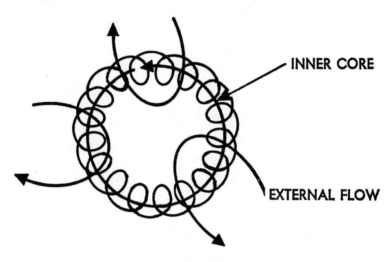

FIGURE XXXI
Vortex Ring Circulation.

It may therefore be assumed that the ether which is interlinked with a vortex ring, will contribute at least a
portion of its mass to the effective mass of the vortex
ring.

Even this, however, will not be sufficient to account for
the total masses of the protons in any known solid or
liquid substance if we assume that the mass of a proton
can come only from the intrinsic mass of the entrained
ether.

The mass of a proton must therefore come almost entirely from some other source, and it may be of gyrostatic
origin, so as to multiply the intrinsic mass of the ether
many times.

If the mass of a proton is somehow the result of its internal motion, then it would seem to follow that the mass of the free ether may likewise be the result of the internal motion or turbulance of the latter, and that a perfectly quiescent ether would be without any mass, and would therefore be non-existent.

If protons and electrons are dipolar vortices in a turbulent ether, then they will be encountered by the ether currents from all directions.

The horizontally approaching ether currents which encounter the dipolar vortex will make the rings increase in diameter, while the vertically approaching ether currents will make them move more closely toward each other.

Exactly the opposite of these two effects will be produced on the dipolar vortex by a dilation of the polar sources, bearing in mind that a proton has more mass than an electron and is therefore more difficult to destroy.

A possible reason why the mass of a proton is greater than that of an electron is that a proton can draw the ether in, throughout its entire periphery, while an electron can draw it in only at the poles.

Since the amount of ether that is sent out, is limited by the amount that can be drawn in, the external ether circulation of a proton must therefore, be greater than that of an electron, provided the sum of the two polar openings is less than the peripheral opening.

Although a positron has the same structural organization as a proton, it has not had sufficient time to acquire any substantial external circulation.

133

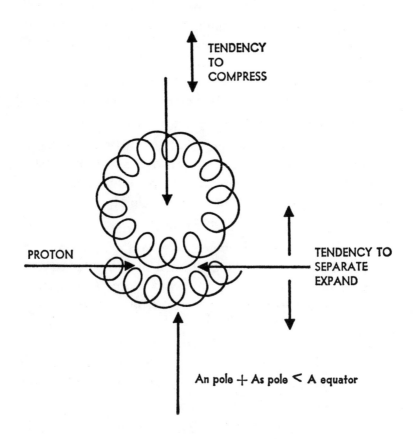

FIGURE XXXII

Forces Acting on Double Vortex.

The change from a positron to a proton may take only a fraction of a second, but it cannot be instantaneous.

It would first have to pass through the various meson stages before it can develop into a completed proton.

Another factor which should be considered, is the Venturi effect.

In the proton, and also in the electron, the externally circulating ether will have to pass through both the peripheral and the polar openings, and if these have different cross-sectional areas, then they will exert a Venturi effect, so that the ether which emerges from the poles of a proton, will have a higher velocity than that which emerges from the periphery of an electron.

Since this external circulating ether must always remain inter-linked with the proton, it must partake of all the movements of the proton, and will therefore contribute its momentum to the proton so as to make the latter more massive than the electron.

This is a necessary consequence of the unique structural organizations of these two particles, and does not depend on any arbitrary assumption that the proton is smaller in size than the electron.

Although two vortex rings can be arranged with rolling contact in either of two different ways, there is only one arrangement possible with three vortex rings because, if the first and second rings are arranged to form a proton, then the second and third will form an electron, or vice versa.

This suggests a structural basis for the neutron, which would then be a single elementary particle smaller and

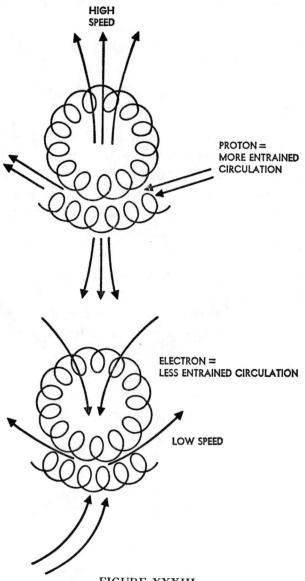

HIGH
SPEED

PROTON =
MORE ENTRAINED
CIRCULATION

ELECTRON =
LESS ENTRAINED CIRCULATION

LOW SPEED

FIGURE XXXIII
Ether Circulation in Proton and Electron.

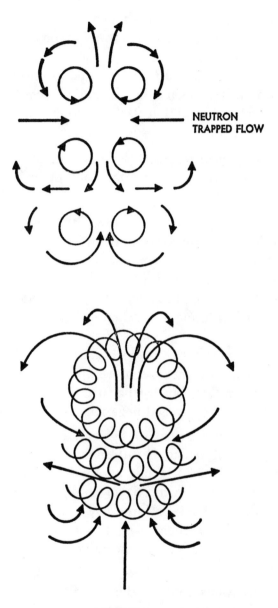

NEUTRON TRAPPED FLOW

FIGURE XXXIV

Circulation in Vortex Neutron

137

more compact than the hydrogen atom, exactly as experimental observations have shown it to be.

Since the vortex neutron has opposite electrifications at its two ends, it should be capable of being polarized, and should readily attach itself to other atoms, both of which are experimentally established facts.

In the vortex neutron, the electron and the proton are not separate entities, but overlap each other in a unique manner.

Such overlapping is possible only with vortex structures and furnishes exactly the kind of structure that is needed to explain not only the compactness and stability of individual neutrons, but also the stability of neutron polymers in the form of inert gas atoms to produce positive ions without entering into chemical combinations.

Under the vortex theory, such inert gas ionization does not take place by the loss of complete electrons, as in chemical ionization, but by the shedding of terminal vortex rings from the exposed negative ends of the neutrons.

Individual neutrons are so light, that when collisions occur, they will rebound, rather than disintegrate; but when they are joined to one another as structural parts of an atom, then the inertia of the entire atom would have to be overcome before they could rebound, and they would then be more likely to shed the terminal vortex rings from their exposed negative ends, so as to form positive ions.

The positive ions thus produced will be of the single proton, or unipolar type; whereas an ordinary chemical bond under the vortex theory, usually comprises a pair of protons arranged as in the hydrogen molecule.

138

When such a positive unipolar ion becomes associated with a negative electron, it will form an atomic oscillator having a structure similar to that of the hydrogen atom.

There is still much uncertainty as to the actual mode of operation of these atomic oscillators, but the vortex theory at least furnishes us with a mechanism which should be capable of radiating or absorbing energy at definite frequencies which is more than can be said of the nuclear theory.

Point-like charges of electricity, floating freely in space, cannot possibly absorb or emit radiation unless they move in definite orbits; and in such case they would radiate all the time and at any frequency.

On the other hand, the vortex does have exactly the required mechanism.

The vortex rings which make up the protons and electrons under the vortex theory, are resilient structures which should themselves be capable of vibrating in various modes, and at different frequencies, as can sometimes be observed in the case of smoke rings.

To account for definite series of spectral lines is not difficult if we have a resilient vibratory structure of this sort to begin with, but nobody has ever offered a satisfactory explanation for spectral lines under the nuclear theory, on the basis of freely floating point-like charges of electricity, which are themselves totally devoid of structure.

However important spectral frequencies may be in our studies of atomic structure, they are not the only messages

139

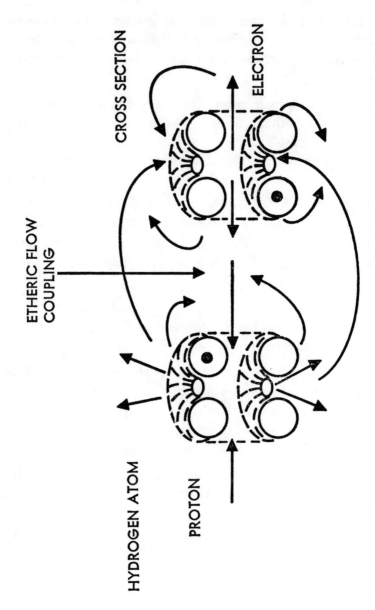

FIGURE XXXV
Hydrogen Atom.

that we get from the insides of atoms, as is often erroneously stated.

All the phenomena of physics and chemistry are messages from the insides of atoms, and the innumerable chemical reactions, each unique in one way or another, give us a much greater variety of information about the insides of atoms than the somewhat restricted information that we get from spectral frequencies.

In fact, the very existence of known chemical elements, and the non-existence of others, gives us information about the structures of the atoms which we could never get from a study of spectral frequencies.

In a structure like the neutron, the outward flow from one of the polar sources, has to escape equatorially through the overlapping electron, which may offer some impediment to such outward flow, and thus reduce the effective mass of the neutron as is evidenced by the mass defects of the atoms which consist entirely, or mainly, of neutrons.

The existence of such a mass defect in the neutron seems to be contradicted by the atomic weight of 1.0089, which the neutron is supposed to have; but we should make allowance for the fact that there is no accurate and direct method available for measuring the mass of the neutron.

A slight mass defect is also found in deuterium, which is to be expected, because the two inwardly facing polar sources of the two protons, oppose each other.

Helium 3 has a mass defect only slightly greater than

141

that of deuterium, whereas helium 4 has a much greater mass defect.

This is significant in that it seems to show that only the nonionizable neutrons on the helium atom are subject to any appreciable mass defect; and since all neutrons and all protons are alike in their stuctures, it must be the position and environment of each neutron and proton in the atom which determines its mass defect.

This relationship of mass defect to position and environment in the atom, if it could be definitely formulated, should lead to a new quantitative check on the structures of the atoms.

On the other hand, we must not lose sight of the fact that the mass defect of helium 3 is approximately the same as that of the deuterium, from which the helium 3 was produced.

This seems to indicate that the mass defect is not determined primarily by the structure of the atom, but that it has been inherited from the precursors of such atoms.

An inspection of the table of packing fractions will show that there is often considerable difference between the mass defects of the different isotopes of the same element, but nowhere do we find as great a difference as between the two isotopes of helium, which seems to show that these are not true isotopes, but different chemical elements.

The mass defects of the atoms increase rapidly along the first horizontal row of the periodic table, and then remain fairly constant, until we get to the neighborhood of tungsten, after which they again diminish, until the end of the periodic table is reached.

142

This means that the average mass of each proton or neutron is lowest throughout the middle portion of the periodic table, but increases toward each end.

The diminution of mass per proton or neutron is especially rapid along the series of elements, from hydrogen to carbon.

There are three, and only three, elementary forces which act at a distance.

Gravitational, electrostatic, and magnetic forces.

It has been argued by the relativists that gravitation should not be included in the same category with electric and magnetic forces, but should be interpreted as a curvature of space, rather than a physical force.

Such an interpretation does not seem to be required by the observed facts, and would only introduce ambiguity and confusion.

Gravitation is a physical force, because it changes the state of rest or motion of material bodies, and therefore requires a physical explanation.

The argument of the relativists, that since gravitation cannot be screened, it must be something intrinsically different from the other forces of nature, is plainly fallacious because the apparent screening of electric and magnetic forces is really neutralization, rather than screening.

Electric and magnetic forces have polarity, and will therefore cause dielectric, or magnetic polarization of the material bodies on which they impinge whereby opposing electric or magnetic forces will be set up, so as to counteract the effects of the original forces.

The reason why no such effect can be produced by the force of gravitation is because gravitation does not have polarity, and not because it is of more fundamental origin than the other forces.

It has also been suggested that gravitation may be due to a slight preponderance of the attractive, over the repulsive, forces between the elementary electric charges.

The difficulty with such an explanation is, that even a small residual effect would still have the same polarization as the original forces, and would therefore be subject to neutralization, or so-called "screening".

It is meaningless to talk about the force of gravity unless there are at least two material bodies, or their equivalents, between which the force is considered as acting.

As a possible equivalent for a material body, there may be substituted a beam of light, which has mass and energy, as evidenced by radiant pressure.

However, we shall confine our attention to two material bodies, preferably about the same size.

There will then be only three theoretical possibilities: they may either attract each other, or repel each other, or have no effect on each other.

If the two bodies were entirely discrete and self contained, they would have no effect upon each other; but it has already been explained that the subatomic particles of which such bodies are composed, probably consist of vortices in the ether which keep the surrounding ether in motion.

144

Except in the immediate neighborhood of its origin, such motion will be random and disorderly, somewhat like the movements of gas molecules, but the moving portions of the ether will be elongated streamers, threads, or jets, rather than pointlike particles.

Those streamers which have the highest velocities will move furthest away from the bodies in which they originated and will eventually encounter the streamers from the other body.

Since the ether is presumably incompressible, these streamers cannot pierce one another, but must be deflected, and the only direction in which such deflection can occur is in the outward radial direction in the common equipotential zone between the two bodies.

The flow patterns of the outwardly directed streamers will therefore be different in the region between the two bodies, than at their remote sides.

In order to compensate for this concentrated outward equatorial flow of the ether in the region between the two bodies, there must be an equivalent inward flow which must occur mainly at the remote sides of each body.

Two material bodies within each other's field of influence will therefore set up a circulatory system of external ether currents similar to that of the electron, but on a much larger scale.

The reverse of this system, which would be similar to that of the proton, can never occur on a large scale because it is only the outwardly directed streamers which will collect in the equipotential zone between the two bodies.

The resultant flow of ether will, therefore, be through

145

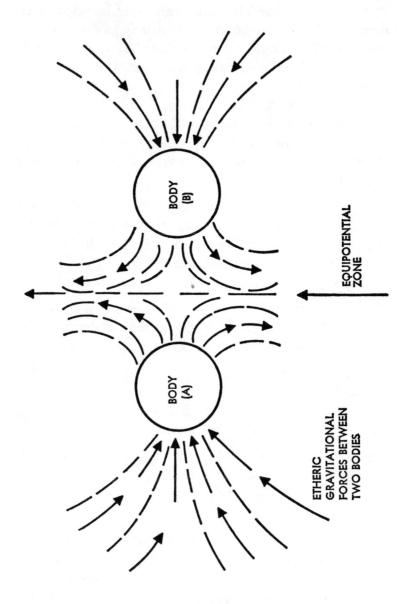

FIGURE XXXVI

Gravitation Flows.

each body, in the direction of the ether, which is probably the cause of the force of gravity, which, according to O. C. Hilgenberg, would require a downward velocity of 2074 kilometers per second, at the surface of the earth.

If gravitation is an ether vortex phenomenon as described above, then the ether in the neighborhood of the earth should be carried along by the earth in its orbital movement about the sun, but should not partake of the rotation of the earth about its axis, because the gravitational field of the earth is bound to, and coordinated with, the gravitational field of the sun.

All of this is in complete agreement with the Sagnac and the Michelson-Gale experiments.

Additional corroboration should be possible with a Foucault pendulum experiment, in which the pendulum is kept swinging, not just for a day or two, but for several months.

If the experiment is performed near the north, or south pole, then the plane in which the pendulum swings, should remain coordinated; not relative to the fixed stars, but relative to the sun so as to make about one revolution a year, relative to the fixed stars.

The astronomical applications of the ether vortex theory will not be discussed here, since there is already an abundant literature on that subject.

See, for instance, the book of E. Ruckhaber (1955).

There is a much closer relationship between electrostatic and magnetic force, than between either of these and gravitation.

147

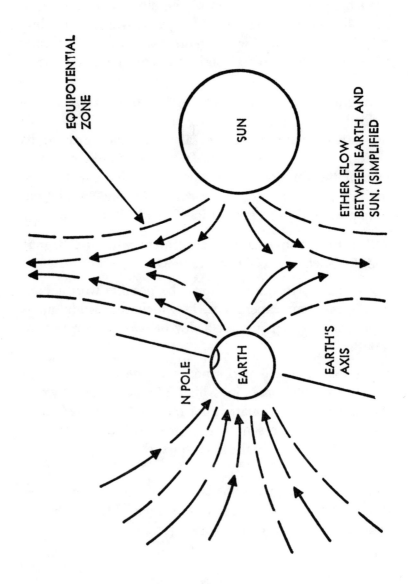

FIGURE XXXVII

Gravity Circulation, Earth to Sun.

Both electrostatic and magnetic forces are polarized; but they differ from each other in that electric poles are complete in themselves, whereas magnetic poles can exist only in pairs, like mirror images.

The distribution of ether currents in the electrostatic field, as contemplated by the vortex theory, is clearly illustrated by the hydrogen atom.

If electrically charged material bodies be substituted for the proton and the electron of the hydrogen atom, then the ether currents which interlink the two charges will still follow the same general course, but on a larger scale.

The polar flow will pass along the axial centerline, from the protons, to the electrons, while the equatorial flow will be on the outside, and in the reverse direction.

The effect of such a closed system of circulation in the space between the protons and the electrons will be to reduce the repulsion caused by the viscidity of the ether, and thus permit such repulsion from the remote sides, to push the protons and the electrons toward each other.

There is, however, a limit to the closeness of their approach to each other, because if they would come into actual contact with each other, their adjacent surfaces would rub each other in opposite directions so as to cause strong repulsion.

This explains why the electrons do not fall completely into the protons.

If, however, two protons are brought very close to each other, their original force of repulsion will change over to a force of attraction, because the contiguous surfaces will then be moving in the same direction.

149

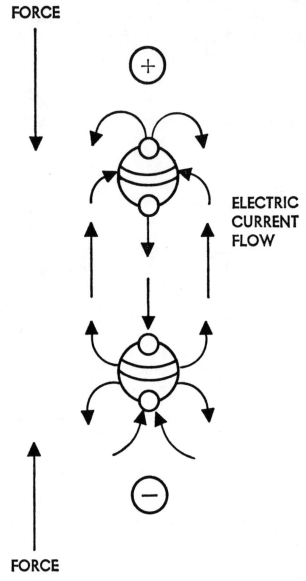

FORCE

ELECTRIC
CURRENT
FLOW

FORCE

FIGURE XXXVIII
Ether Circulation From Electric Charges.

Such a force of attraction was discovered experimentally in 1936, and has been designated as "super-gravitation".

Although protons and electrons are symmetrical bipolar structures, there seems to be no reason why the external ether circulation should have to pass through both poles simultaneously, and in equal amounts.

Thus, when an electron is electrically coupled with a proton, the interlinked ether currents will probably follow the shortest path, and remain connected with only those poles which face each other, and are nearest to each other.

In the physics literature of today, the magnetic field is usually considered as consisting of magnetic lines of force extending circumferentially or spirally around the current carrying wire, or passing out of the north pole and into the south pole of a magnet.

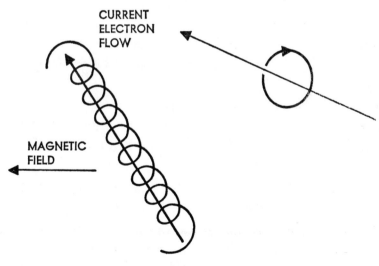

CURRENT
ELECTRON
FLOW

MAGNETIC
FIELD

FIGURE XXXIX
Magnetic Field.

151

The magnetic line of force itself is usually interpreted as the locus of some medium or agency which causes magnetic action at a distance, and which must, therefore, be endowed with physical reality.

However useful such a concept may be for making practical calculations, these magnetic lines of force are merely mathematical fictions, completely devoid of physical reality.

If they would have physical reality, then the question would immediately arise as to why their direction is always left-handed, and never right-handed, relative to the direction of movement of the electrons.

Is it possible that the ether in which they exist, may be internally twisted, or that the electrons themselves may have asymmetric structures?

Such assumptions seem so highly improbable that we feel compelled to look for some other explanation.

The force of magnetism seems to have its origin in the forces of attraction or repulsion between electric currents flowing in the same, or in opposite directions, respectively.

If the electric currents are along circular paths, then the magnetic effect will appear in the form of magnetic poles which are either N or S poles, depending on the side from which we view the electric currents.

It necessarily follows that there can never be a single isolated magnetic pole.

All of this is clearly understood in the theoretical physics of today, but the difficulty is in explaining why there will be such attractive or repulsive forces between electric currents.

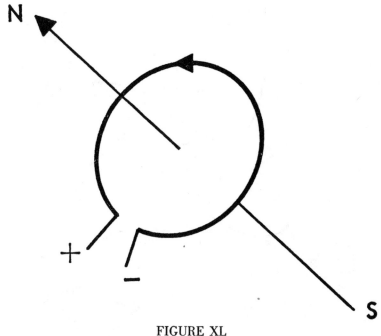

FIGURE XL

Magnetic Field Around Loop.

A simple example of an electric current, is the flow of electrons in a copper wire.

The ether currents which keep the moving electrons connected with the protons of the copper atoms, will then become extended lengthwise of the wire, and will keep the moving electrons oriented in the same direction.

The polar flow of ether from the protons to the electrons, will then be in the direction of movement of the electrons, while the external return flow (which constitutes the true magnetic field) will be in the reverse direction, in the space around the wire.

When the wire has the form of a solenoid, the surround-

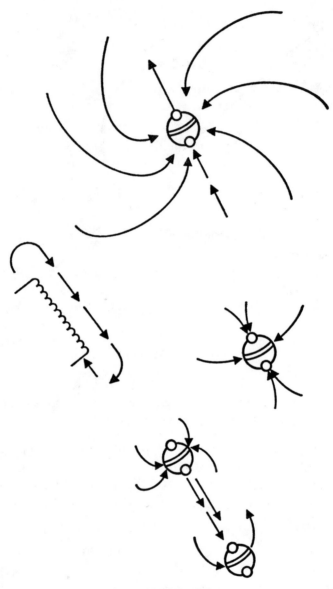

FIGURE XLI

Magnetic Coupling.

ing ether will therefore circulate in a direction OP-POSITE to the direction of travel of the electrons, and not in the same direction as would be expected under the nuclear theory, if the ether were considered as being merely carried along by the moving electrons.

The above conclusion as to the direction of flow of the ether in the magnetic field is a necessary consequence of the vortex structures which have been ascribed to protons and electrons respectively.

If these structures would be reversed, then the direction of flow of the ether in the magnetic field would also be reversed.

That our choice of structures has been correct seems to be corroborated, not only by the direction of the induced electromotive force in electromagnetic induction, but also by the direction of the magneto-optic effect.

All organic substances, and nearly all inorganic substances, when placed in a magnetic field, will rotate the plane of polarization of light in a direction OPPOSITE to the direction of movement of the electrons in the solenoidal current around the magnet.

There are only a few inorganic substances ($FeCl_3$ for example) which are exceptions, and these exceptional cases are probably due to some stroboscopic effect.

The direction of induced electromotive force also leads to the same conclusion as to the direction of flow of the ether in the magnetic field.

When a current is started, or increased, in the primary circuit, the induced current in the secondary will flow

155

in the OPPOSITE direction, which seems to indicate that the free electrons in the secondary are given an impulse in a direction opposite to the direction of movement of the electrons in the primary.

Such an impulse can be imparted only by a magnetic field around the primary and seems to consist of a sudden flow of ether in a direction opposite to the direction of movement of the electrons in the primary.

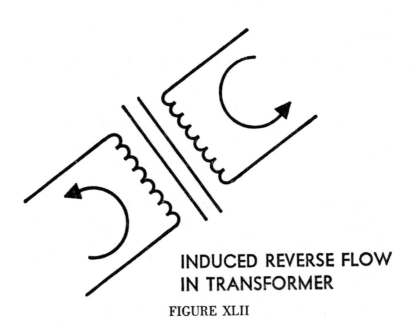

INDUCED REVERSE FLOW
IN TRANSFORMER

FIGURE XLII

The induced current in the secondary will continue to flow only as long as the acceleration of the electrons continues.

After the current in the primary no longer increases in strength, there will no longer be any induced electromotive force in the secondary, but the free elctrons in the secondary will still be held in their oriented positions by the magnetic field.

If the current in the primary then diminishes or stops flowing, the magnetic field will be removed from the secondary, and the free electrons which were held in oriented positions by such a magnetic field, will be released, whereupon they will spring back into their natural positions which will constitute a flow of current in the same direction as the current in the primary.

Electromagnetic induction therefore leads to the same conclusions as the magneto-optic effect in regard to the direction of flow of the ether in the magnetic field.

It will be seen from the foregoing that it is the same external flow of ether from the electrons, to the protons, which forms both the electrostatic, and the magnetic field.

In the electrostatic field, however, these external ether currents, emerge from, and terminate upon electrically charged particles, whereas in the magnetic field, they flow in closed circuits; either along the path of an electric circuit, or around the periphery of a magnet.

The reason why an electrostatic charge does not exert any force upon a magnetic pole, is because a magnetic pole is electrically neutral.

It does not contain an accumulation of one kind of electricity, and therefore behaves toward an electric charge in the same manner as any other metal body would behave.

Since the ether around an electric charge does not flow in closed circuits, but only from the electrons to the

157

protons, any force which this unidirectional flow of ether may exert upon half of the magnetic pole, would be counterbalanced by an equal, and opposite force, upon the other half.

Although an electric charge and a magnetic pole do not exert any force upon each other, they do act upon each other.

The electric charge will induce an equal and opposite charge on the adjacent surface of the magnetic pole, while the magnetic pole will induce unidirectional orientation of the electrons, relative to the protons, in the electrically charged body; just as in any other body which is positioned in a magnetic field.

If the body is transparent, then such orientation can be detected by the magneto-optic effect.

Electric and magnetic fields differ from the gravitational field in that the flow of ether in electric and magnetic fields is always confined to limited regions.

It either passes from negative to positive charges, around a closed circuit, whereas in a gravitational field the ether merely passes through any body that is in its path.

That is the reason why all efforts to screen or otherwise control the gravitational field have been unsuccessful.

If this could ever be accomplished, then a simple system of interplanetary travel would probably be possible.

The problem, however, is not entirely hopeless. The very fact that the gravitational field acts more effectively on protons, than upon electrons, seems to show that gravitational ether currents do coact in some specific manner with electrically charged particles, and when we determine the manner in which they coact, then we shall be in a better position to solve the problem of an easy method of interplanetary travel.

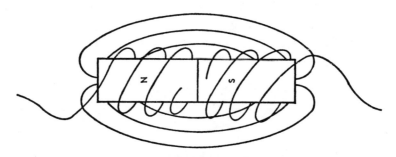

FIGURE XLIII

Flow Around Permanent Magnet.

The Superposition of Elementary Fields of Force

With the exception of radiant pressure, there are only three elementary forces which act at a distance; gravitational, electrostatic, and magnetic forces.

The ether-vortex theory seems to furnish the answer as to how three such forces can act independently of each other in the same space and at the same time.

According to the latest views, the force of gravity is caused by a pressure of the ether, rather than by a movement thereof.

If there is present only one body, and it is spherical in form, then from considerations of symmetry, it follows that the ether will be in the same condition on all sides of the body.

159

If, however, there are two bodies close to each other, as in the case of a double star, then the condition of spherical symmetry will no longer exist, but instead, there will only be axial symmetry.

The ether currents of the two bodies will then organize themselves into the form of a dipolar vortex, similar to the field around an electron; but on a much larger scale.

The effect of this vortex will be to create a difference in pressure on the proximate and remote sides of the two bodies.

The ether in the space between the two bodies will be at a lower pressure than at their remote sides; and such a difference in pressure will push the two bodies toward each other, and cause them to fall into each other, unless they are in orbital movement about each other, so that centrifugal force will keep them apart.

GRAVITY
= ETHERIC PRESSURE

ELECTRIC AND MAGNETIC
= MOVEMENT OF ETHER IN
WHIRLS AND EDDIES

Electric and magnetic forces are caused, not by pressure of the ether, but by movement of the ether in the form of whirls, or eddies.

These exist on a much smaller scale and are more localized than gravitational fields of force.

Since whirls and eddies can exist regardless of the pressure of the ether, it is readily seen why electric and magnetic forces can act independently of gravitational force; and vice versa.

There now remains only the superposition of electric and magnetic fields upon each other, either coaxially, or transversely of each other (as we have in the Great Pyramid).

In this consideration, let us consider first, their coaxial superposition.

An electrostatic field consists of a flow of ether in a direct line from protons in the positive electrode, to electrons in the negative electrode, and then back again to the protons through outside paths.

If the electrodes are made of iron, and are magnetized, with the N and S poles facing each other, then the magnetic field will consist of a rotation of the ether around their axis of symmetry; and such a rotating or spinning movement of the ether can occur simultaneously with the circulatory movement that corresponds to the electrostatic field.

A magnetic field, can, therefore, be superimposed directly upon a coaxial electrostatic field.

If the magnetic field is superimposed transversely upon the electrostatic field, then both fields will be distorted, but not destroyed.

The circulating ether which constitutes the electrostatic field will no longer retain its axial symmetry, but it will, nevertheless, continue to circulate.

161

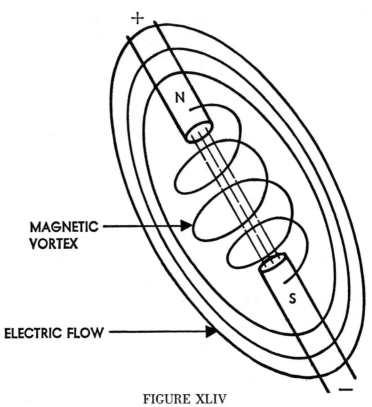

FIGURE XLIV
Superimposed Fields.

Similarly, the rotating ether which constitutes the magnetic field, will pursue irregular and non-circular paths; but it will continue to rotate.

A magnetic field can, therefore, be superimposed transversely in any direction upon an electrostatic field, without interfering with the latter.

An example of the transverse field effect is demonstrated in pyramid power.

Figure XLV is an example.

162

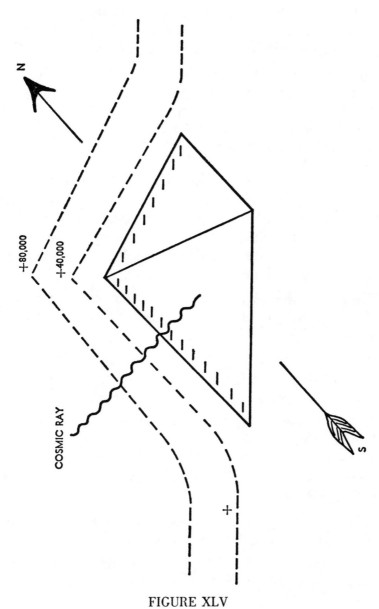

FIGURE XLV
Superimposed Forces on Pyramid.

163

In this case, there is a shaped electrostatic field due to the structure of the pyramid, and the action of the earth's magnetic field on the resultant shaped ether flow.

The result of these effects would be the formation of a rather large ether vortex in the pyramid.

The ether-vortex casts some interesting probabilities on possible interplanetary travel.

Merely because present-day methods of propulsion conists of rotary propellers, jet, and rocket propulsion, is no reason why some electric or magnetic device cannot be employed, for, besides the force of counteracting the force of gravity, there is also the problem of producing enormous accelerations.

These two problems are so closely related that solution of one of them would probably also be a solution to the other.

In all methods of propulsion that we are familiar with, a mechanical force is exerted upon a physical object, so as to counteract its weight, its inertia, or both.

This is, however, far from satisfactory, since there is a limit to what can be done in free space on an unsupported object, by the application of externally applied forces, and the limit has almost been reached in jet planes and rockets.

Greater forces could be applied, but only at the expense of greater loads of fuel that would have to be carried.

Some other method will have to be found before we can hope to undertake interplanetary travel.

Gravitational forces and inertial forces are due to interaction between material bodies and the ether.

Instead of trying to control a body by acting upon it directly, it may be possible to control it more effectively by acting upon the ether, which in turn controls the behavior of the body.

Students of aikido and ju-jitsu would understand such a reaction, for it is quite similar.

A change in the state of rest, or motion, of a body is always caused by a difference of ether pressure on opposite sides of the body.

Thus, in the case of two celestial bodies which attract each other gravitationally, the ether pressure in the space between them is less than on their remote sides.

Such a difference of pressure could be neutralized if some of the ether could be transformed from the high pressure side to the low pressure side.

Since the ether is a fluid, it should be capable of being moved from one place to another.

An ordinary bar magnet will not serve this purpose because the North and South poles are mirror images of each other; it being now well established that the ether circulates around the magnet, and not out of one pole and into another.

If a series of magnets be arranged end-to-end so as to form a closed ring, there will be an external ether circulation, similar in form to a smoke ring.

If two of these cores be placed face-to-face against each other, in such a manner that their circulating ether currents are in rolling contact; that is, in rolling contact with each other, they will form a large scale replica of either

165

the vortex proton, or the vortex electron; depending on whether the ether in the space between them flows inwardly, or outwardly.

A similar transfer of ether is also produced by an electrostatic condenser.

If protons and electrons are dipolar vortices with two vortex rings in rolling contact with each other, then in a charged condenser there will be a unidirectional flow of ether from the protons of the positive charge, to the electrons of the negative charge; the return flow being either around the edges of the plates, or between the molecules of the dielectric.

These magnetic and electrostatic devices can be combined in many different ways.

By the proper arrangement, and by the use of personal controls, it should be possible to maintain a regulated flow of ether through such a system in any direction; into or out of it, so as to change the ether pressure in and around the system.

Perhaps the Egyptians used such a system to transport the huge blocks of stone in the Great Pyramid.

A comment will probably be that such a system would be contrary to the law of conservation of energy; a violation of the first law of thermodynamics.

This law, however, applies only to isolated systems, and a process which involves the transfer of ether to and from the outside, is hardly an isolated system.

There is much we still do not know about the law of conservation of energy.

In spite of all the glamour of modern technology, the orthodox science of today is still unable to draw a single plausible picture, or diagram, of even the simplest elementary particle, or to give any intelligible explanation for any of the forces that act at a distance.

The ether-vortex theory would give us a new method of approach, and may open up a new field for experimental research.

First, we should try to find some method of producing regions of increased, or decreased, ether pressure, and then study the effect of such conditions upon the elementary particles of matter.

If we merely continue along the present lines of thought, then the problem of producing an anti-gravity device will probably never be solved.

It may be troublesome to change over from a nucleated atom to a vortex atom, but it will be still more troublesome ten or twenty years from now, and eventually the change will have to be made, for there is a continually increasing amount of evidence that is piling up against the nuclear theory.

It is significant that the physics profession has never made any effort to attack the new vortex theory of the atom.

Any evidence that can be produced in support of the nuclear theory is equally applicable to the vortex theory, and the latter can explain many things which the nuclear theory cannot explain at all.

It is only the vortex theory which has been able to offer any suggestions as to how we may proceed in our efforts to solve the problems of biocosmic energy and of anti-gravity.

There should be no place in real scientific effort for dogma, for where there is dogma, there is little freedom for inquiry, and when free inquiry is stifled there is much error in the secrecy that stifles it.

Today, we quite accept all the comforts and luxuries that electrical energy, and its mechanical devices, have made possible for us to enjoy.

We seldom, if ever, give a thought to the fact that behind all these comforts we take for granted lies some seven generations of effort by men whose purpose in life was to bring these achievements to hundreds of millions yet unborn.

For all those men and women of a future day, there are those among us today who are laboring toward other advances which will assist them to more abundant living.

Of one thing you may be certain; there is a continuous chain of improvement over the ages, and it is the wish of the author that you, too, enter into this spirit of evolutionary progress toward greater and more abundant enlightenment in your time, for in this vibrating world all things can be reconciled.

FINIS

REFERENCES

1. ——————, *Kybalion*. Chicago: Yogi Publication Society, 1930.

2. Verlag, H., *The Power of Breath*. Whittier, California. Doty Trade Press, 1958.

3. Yogi Ramacharaka, *Science of Breath*. Chicago: Yoga Publication Society, 1904.

4. Rele, Vasant G., *The Mysterious Kundalini*. Bombay, India: D. B. Taraporala Sons, 1960.

5. Bernard, Raymond, *The Serpent Fire*. Mokelumne Hill, Cal.: Health Research, 1959.

6. David-Neel, Alexandra, *Magic and Mystery in Tibet*. Baltimore: Penguin Books, 1929.

7. Moss, Louis, M.D., *Acupuncture and You*. New York: Dell, 1964.

8. Chan, Pedro, *Acupuncture and Electro-acupuncture*. Alhambra, Cal.: Borden, 1972.

9. Palos, Stephen, *Chinese Art of Healing*. New York City: Bantam Books, 1963.

10. Mann, Felix, *Acupuncture*. New York: Vintage, 1962.

11. Steiger, Brad, *Secrets of Kahuna Magic*. New York: Award Books, 1971.

12. Long, Max Freedom, *Secret Science at Work*. Los Angeles: DeVorss, 1953.

13. Hall, Manly P., *The Mystical and Medical Philosophy of Paracelsus*. Los Angeles: Philosophical Research Society, 1964.

14. Reichenbach, Baron Karl von, *Letters on Od and Magnetism*. Mokelumne Hill, Cal.: Health Research, 1851, reprinted 1967.

15. Babbitt, Edwin G., *Principles of Light and Color*. New York: University Books, 1967. (reprint of 1895 book)

16. Russ, Charles Dr., "An Instrument Which Is Set In Motion by Vision or by Proximity of the Human Body," *The Lancet*, 30 July, 1921, P. 222.

17. Lakhovsky, George. *The Secret of Life*. Mokelumne Hill, Ca.: Health Research, 1939.

18. Ostrander and Schroeder, *Psychic Discoveries Behind the Iron Curtain*. New Jersey: Prentice Hall, 1971.

19. Tompkins, Peter, *Secrets of the Great Pyramid*. New York: Harper and Row, 1971.

20. Private communication.

21. Private communication.

22. Tiller, Wm. A. Ph.D., "Radionics, Radiethesia and Physics," *Transcript of Symposium*, 30 October, 1971. The Academy of Para-Psychology and Medicine, Los Altos, Ca.

169

23. Beal, James B. "Recent Developments Associated with Bio-electric Field," unpublished. 4209 Fortson, Huntsville, Alabama 35810.

24. Beal, James B. "The New Bio-technology," unpublished. Same as above.

25. Feynman, Richard P., *Lectures on Physics*. Palo Alto, Ca.: Addison-Wesley Inc., 1964.

26. Pressman, Dr. A. S., *Electromagnetic Fields and Life*. New York: Plenum Press, 1970.

27. Hardy, Dr. J. D., *Physiological Problems in Space Exploration*. Springfield: Yale University Medical School, 1971.

28. Benavides, Rodolfo, *Dramatic Profecies of the Great Pyramid*. Mexico: Graficos Olimpo, 1970.

29. Capt, Raymond E., *The Great Pyramid Decoded*. Thousand Oaks, Cal.: Artisan Sales, 1970.

30. Eepic, Emil, *The Imminent Shift of the Earth's Axis*. Eureka, Cal.: Sepic, 1960.

31. Flanagan, G. P., *The Pyramid and Its Relationship to Biocosmic Energy*. Los Angeles: Laser Sound, 1971.

32. Private interview with Jose Silva, founder of Silva Mind Control.

33. Hieronymus, Galen, *Tracking the Astronauts in Apollo* 11. Lakemont, Ga.: Advanced Sciences Development and Research Assn., P.O. Box 77, Lakemont, Ga. 30052.

34. Day, Langston, *Matter in the Making*. London: Vincent Stuart Ltd., 1966.

INDEX

M

Magnetic experiments, 39, 66
Magnetic fields, 39, 109, 143, 147, 151-157
Magnetic poles, 147
Magnetic vortex, 165, 166
Magneto-optic effect, 155-158
Malebranche, Nicolas; 128
Mana, 11
Mass defect, 141-143
Maxwell, James Clerk; 111
Measuring devices, 95-105
Meson, 135
Metric system, 60
Michelson, A. A.; 109, 121
Michaelson-Gale experiment, 110, 121, 122, 147
Michaelson-Morley experiment, 110, 120, 121
Milk preservation, 23, 49
Mitogenic rays, 15, 18, 34
Momentum, 119
Motion, concept of; 118, 119
Mummification, 21, 49, 66, 85, 86

N

Nature, 109
Negative ions, 47-48
Neurophone, 27-35, 39, 49
Neutrons, 109, 128; neutron structure, 135, 138
Newton, Isaac; 111, 112, 123

O

Odic force, 13-14
Orbital velocity of earth, 122
Oxygen, 3, 20, 48, 71

P

Paracelsus, 13
Pavlita, Robert, 25, 26, 91
Pendulum, 103
Periodic table, 142
Photons, 119, 124
Physics, theoretical, 108
Pineal gland, 5
Planck, Max, 124
Polar shift, 64
Positron, 133
Prana, 3, 4, 20, 48

Protons, 109, 128, 130; proton structure, 130-134, 166
Psychotronic energy, 25, 26, 98, 103; psychotronic twirler, 91-94
Pyramid, alignment, 63, 64; effect on animals, 81; effect on foods, 124-128; effect on plants, 86-88
Pyramid energy plate, 91
Pyramid mathematics, 51-62
Pyramid matrix or grid, 88-91
Pyramid of Gizeh, 21, 48, 50, 51-62, 63, 162, 166; measurements, 56
Pyramid power, 21-24, 25
Pyramid, subjective response, 80-82
Pyramid vortex, 162
Pyramid windows, ventilation, 63, 81

Q

Qi, 11
Quanta, energy, 124
Quintessence, 13

R

Razor blade sharpener, 24, 66
Red shift, 116
Reichenbach, Baron Karl von, 13
Relativity, 121
Resonance, 28-30, 35

S

Sacred cut . . . see Golden Section
Sagnac experiment, 110, 121, 147
Semi-conductor effect, 37, 75, 76
Sleep, 47
Smoke rings, 139, 165
Spectral lines, 139
Stethnometer, 16
Stokes, George, 111, 121
Super-gravitation, 151
Superposition of electric and magnetic forces, 161-165

T

Tch'i. 9, 37, 94
Third eye, 5
Tibet, 7, 81
Tobiscope, 36
Transmutation, 13
Tumo, 7, 9, 81, 94